M000087866

Contents

Opening the COMMON CORE

HOW TO BRING **ALL** STUDENTS TO COLLEGE AND CAREER READINESS

CAROL CORBETT BURRIS • DELIA T. GARRITY

CORWIN

A SAGE Company

CORWIN
A SAGE Company

FOR INFORMATION:

Corwin
A SAGE Company
2455 Teller Road
Thousand Oaks, California 91320
(800) 233-9936
www.corwin.com

SAGE Publications Ltd.
1 Oliver's Yard
55 City Road
London EC1Y 1SP
United Kingdom

SAGE Publications India Pvt. Ltd.
B 1/I 1 Mohan Cooperative Industrial Area
Mathura Road, New Delhi 110 044
India

SAGE Publications Asia-Pacific Pte. Ltd.
3 Church Street
#10-04 Samsung Hub
Singapore 049483

Acquisitions Editor: Dan Alpert
Associate Editor: Megan Bedell
Editorial Assistant: Sarah Bartlett
Production Editor: Amy Schroller
Copy Editor: Diane DiMura
Typesetter: C&M Digitals (P) Ltd.
Proofreader: Dennis Webb
Indexer: Judy Hunt
Cover Designer: Lisa Riley
Permissions Editor: Karen Ehrmann

Copyright © 2012 by Corwin

Printed in the United States of America

Library of Congress Cataloging-in-Publication Data

Burris, Carol Corbett.

Opening the common core : how to bring all students to college and career readiness / Carol Corbett Burris, Delia T. Garrity.

p. cm.
Includes bibliographical references and index.

ISBN 978-1-4522-2623-1 (pbk.)

1. College preparation programs--United States. 2. School-to-work transition--United States. I. Garrity, Delia T. II. Title.

LB2351.2.B87 2012
378.1′610973—dc23   2012001336

This book is printed on acid-free paper.

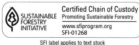

SUSTAINABLE FORESTRY INITIATIVE
Certified Chain of Custody
Promoting Sustainable Forestry
www.sfiprogram.org
SFI-01268
SFI label applies to text stock

12 13 14 15 16 10 9 8 7 6 5 4 3 2 1

Foreword

Twenty-five years ago, two prominent reports urged policymakers to move toward educator professionalization (Carnegie Forum on Education and the Economy, 1986; Holmes Group, 1986). Students, these reports reasoned, "are better served by teachers who are prepared to make responsible decisions and then given the authority to do so" (Darling-Hammond & Wise, 1992, p. 1359). By the mid-1990s, however, it was clear that state and national policy was heading in the opposite direction. Assessments were put in place to measure students' progress toward meeting newly instituted performance standards aligned to curriculum standards. The rationale for the carefully aligned standards-based reforms was sound—no longer would schools suffer with conflicting, disorganized mandates for change. No longer would some schools set much lower standards than others.

But among the unintended, undesirable consequences that have arisen from these reforms has been a double whammy for educators—less discretion coupled with more responsibility. That is, the standards-based reform movement has resulted in a vicious and untoward blaming of teachers and principals for outcomes that they cannot fully control. Further, it has pushed those educators to maintain a laser-like focus on the measured outcomes and on the tests themselves—narrowing curriculum and teaching to the tests—all in order to achieve a set of goals that often feel only tangentially related to the reasons why the they entered the profession.

While these trends show few signs of fading, educators can take heart in this new book from Carol Burris and Delia Garrity. Even during a time when policy has been dominated by standards and testing policies, they helped lead their district—Rockville Centre, in Long Island, New York—toward teaching and learning grounded in the development of teachers as knowledgeable, trusted professionals. The results of their efforts are well documented—a remarkable increase in both excellence and equity. Despite the cacophony of mandates and sanctions, they have focused on what really matters—providing all students with excellent and challenging learning experiences that are deep, meaningful, preparatory, and not driven by testing.

Burris and Garrity note at the book's outset the ongoing adoption and implementation of the Common Core State Standards (CCSS) throughout the nation. In fact, they embrace these standards. Because they do so, the book serves as a crucial missing element to the CCSS, guiding policymakers on how to move from the standards toward practices shown to increase learning and thus move students closer to meeting those standards. Similarly, the details illustrated throughout the book provide educators with corresponding tools—ways to move forward in a standards-based policy context.

This book provides a pathway for the CCSS to be something more than the *same old same old* for educators. Maybe, if we are wise and careful this time, the path does not necessarily have to lead to the well worn and cruel "just do it, no excuses" condemnations. Perhaps teachers and principals can thrive as professionals, with students reaping the learning rewards.

Burris and Garrity, in this new book, explain what it will take to do it. They help unpack the standards and describe, through examples and lessons, how to give all students more enriched learning experiences that will better prepare them for the 21st century. They wisely caution that the old drill and skill practices that are often resorted to by pressured teachers with struggling students are not the most effective ways to improve learning. The authors share research on the effectiveness of an accelerated approach, and they give the reader strategies on implementation. Indeed, they provide throughout the book practical suggestions that teachers can use with their most vulnerable students to make sure that those students are included and not relegated to the sidelines of education. The spirit of their first book, *Detracking for Excellence and Equity*, can be found throughout this second work, especially in the chapter that focuses specifically on equity.

For the past eight years, I have been blessed with the opportunity to study Rockville Centre's reforms and to work with Carol Burris on that research. I have seen the dedication of Burris, Garrity, Superintendent William Johnson, and their instructional staff. I have seen that dedication pay off as the district's large achievement gap has narrowed tremendously, with overall achievement rising and Burris's high school gaining repeated recognition as one of the best in the nation. Challenging, engaging, supported learning is not a secret formula; the National Research Council and the Institute of Medicine (2004), among many others, have explained these essential elements in detail. But what Burris, Garrity, and others in Rockville Centre have done is take that formula and make it part of their— and their students'—daily lives. This book explains how they did this and how others can do the same.

This is an overwhelming time for our nation's teachers, as they feel the brunt of national and state policies motivated by callous political agendas. Burris and Garrity give teachers and school leaders practical, useful tools grounded in experience and in research. The tools are offered as a way for educators to implement change in a way that reminds us all of what reform should really be about, in the words of John Dewey (1879), "that education is the fundamental method of social progress and reform" (p. 79). And a lot of what it takes is improving learning opportunities through improved, more equitable, and more supported schools.

Professor Kevin G. Welner
Director, National Education Policy Center
School of Education
University of Colorado Boulder

Preface

The Common Core State Standards (National Governors Association, 2010) represent a dramatic shift in beliefs about the purposes of American schooling. If all students are to achieve the Common Core State Standards, schools must thoughtfully and thoroughly reexamine and change curriculum, instruction, and school structures. This book provides concrete suggestions to help schools achieve this goal.

This book provides a comprehensive approach that integrates the standards of the Core with strategies that ensure that equity is front and center as schools and teachers engage in Core implementation. The authors provide practical strategies that teachers can use based on four essential principles—acceleration, critical thinking, equity, and support (ACES)—in order to transform instruction to meet the requirements of the new standards. These strategies are applied and developed in model lessons linked to Common Core and Knowledge and Skills for University Success (KSUS) standards.

This book is designed to serve as a guide to K–12 educators, both teachers and school leaders, who wish to redesign learning experiences so that all of their students, including their English language learners and students with disabilities, will not be left behind as they seek to bring all students to college and career readiness.

Acknowledgments

Corwin gratefully acknowledges the contributions of the following reviewers:

Michele Badovinac, Director
AVID Region 6
San Joaquin County Office of Education
Stockton, CA

Damon Douglas, Math and ELA Curriculum Specialist
Northampton, MA

Cathy French, Mathematics Coordinator
Hazelwood School District
Florissant, MO

Michael Horton, AVID Administrator
Riverside County Office of Education
Riverside, CA

Jeff Ronneberg, Superintendent
Spring Lake Park, MN

Debbie Zacarian, Director
Center for English Language Education and Center for Advancing Student
   Achievement at the Collaborative for Educational Services
Northampton, MA

About the Authors

Carol Corbett Burris has served as principal of South Side High School in the Rockville Centre School District in New York since 2000. Prior to becoming a principal, she was a teacher at both the middle and high school level. She received her doctorate from Teachers College, Columbia University, and her dissertation, which studied her district's detracking reform in math, received the 2003 National Association of Secondary School Principals' Middle Level Dissertation of the Year Award. In 2010, she was named the New York State Outstanding Educator by School Administrators Association of New York State.

She is the coauthor, with Delia Garrity, of *Detracking for Excellence and Equity*. Articles that she has authored or coauthored have appeared in *Educational Leadership*, *The Kappan*, the *American Educational Research Journal*, *The Teachers College Record*, *Theory Into Practice*, *The School Administrator*, the *American School Board Journal*, and *EdWeek*. A chapter on closing the achievement gap, which she coauthored with Kevin Welner, appeared in *Lessons in Integration: Realizing the Promise of Racial Diversity in America's Schools*, a volume edited by the Harvard Civil Rights Project. She can be reached at burriscarol@gmail.com.

Delia T. Garrity was a public school educator for thirty-seven years, serving as a math teacher, teacher of the gifted, mathematics department chairperson, curriculum supervisor, assistant principal, and assistant superintendent. During her tenure as assistant superintendent for curriculum and instruction in Rockville Centre School District, New York, she provided the leadership in opening academic doors to all students and designed a comprehensive professional learning model for teachers and administrators. As assistant principal of South Side Middle School in Rockville Centre, Delia facilitated the school's transformation from a tracked system to one that offers an honors curriculum in heterogeneous classes for all students. She received the New York State Middle School Assistant Principal of the Year Award in 1996. She has taught graduate courses on mathematics education at Long Island University and is a guest lecturer at Teachers College, Columbia University. She is a national educational consultant and presenter who works with educators to create equitable, heterogeneous classrooms where each student, including special education students, English language learners, and gifted students receive the same high quality, rich education. She coauthored *Detracking for Excellence and Equity* with Carol C. Burris and authored or coauthored articles in *American School Board Journal, The School Administrator,* and *The Arithmetic Teacher.* Delia can be reached at dtgarrity@gmail.com.

Introduction

*Over the next 10 years, nearly half of all new jobs will require educa-
tion that goes beyond a high school education. . . . And so the question
is whether all of us—as citizens, and as parents—are willing to do
what's necessary to give every child a chance to succeed.*

President Barack Obama,
State of the Union Address, January 25, 2011

Each year, nearly two-thirds of all high school graduates enter postsecondary education as the first step in their adult lives. This is a wise
choice given the highly competitive marketplace of the 21st century. As
noted in President Obama's 2011 State of the Union Address quoted
above, a high school diploma is no longer enough to compete in the new
economy.

This was not always the case. During the first half of the 20th century,
a high school diploma was a satisfying achievement as well as a sound
credential for successful employment and economic security. During the
21st century, however, a high school diploma without further training provides far fewer options for young adults. High school graduates have an
unemployment rate of 32 percent—twice that of college graduates (Dillon,
2009). In addition, college graduates earn 74 percent more than their coun-
terparts with only a high school diploma (Ames, 2010). Clearly, in our
present economy, postsecondary education has become a necessity, not
merely an attractive option.

This is in part because technology has changed everything. When it
comes to securing jobs, our students not only compete with their classmates, they compete on an international playing field as well. In a single
generation, revolutions in technology have transformed the way we live,
work, and do business. Because of technology, steel mills once manned by
one thousand workers now only need one hundred, and the Internet

allows anyone anywhere in the world to produce and sell products to a global market (Obama, 2011). Video conferencing and faster and more prevalent Internet connections will only accelerate this trend in years to come.

If American students face international competition for jobs, it makes sense to compare how they do in college with the college performance of students around the world. The Organization for Economic Cooperation and Development (OECD) is an alliance of industrialized countries whose mission is to promote economic growth and engage in research. One topic of interest is the educational level of its member countries' citizens. Of the twenty-nine member nations of the OECD, the American college completion rate, defined as the rate of completion for those who begin college studies, is now below the OECD average, ranking 13th. What is equally as troubling, however, is that the United States has the lowest college completion growth rate of all OECD nations. Between 1995 and 2006, the postsecondary education completion rate for Finland's students grew from 28 percent to 48 percent. Australia's rate increased from 36 percent in 2000 to 59 percent in 2006. The American yearly college completion rate, however, has hardly budged—in 1995 it was 33 percent and eleven years later it was 36 percent (OECD, 2009). In fact, our nation's college dropout rate was the highest among OECD countries in 2006 (College Board, 2009).

Although there may be a variety of reasons why students drop out of college, preparation is a factor that must be considered. Among OECD members, our students rank below average in reading, mathematics, and literacy. Problem solving, a skill needed to be successful in college and the workplace, is the capacity to understand problems in unique situations, develop effective solutions, and solve and communicate possible solutions to others. In this very important skill, American students ranked 24th of the 29 participating countries (OECD, 2004). Half of all American students failed to demonstrate these problem-solving skills that the OECD considers necessary to meet the needs of the 21st century workforce (College Board, 2009).

If you dig deeper, you find that behind the average scores, there is also tremendous divide in American student performance. Even as some American students do extraordinarily well, even more do extraordinarily poorly. The proportion of American students who performed at the highest level of proficiency on the 2006 Program for International Student Assessment (PISA) of the OECD, was 9 percent, which is a little above the OECD average. However, there is a far larger proportion of students at the lowest level—24 percent. In fact, the United States is the only OECD country that has a large percentage of performers at the top and a large percentage at the bottom (College Board, 2009). And therein lies the problem. As this and other PISA results show, we prepare some students very well, but others are dismally neglected. We simply do not provide the same challenging and enriched educational experience for all students.

Our society can no longer afford to have educational *haves and have nots*. Although ultimately not all students will attend college, every child has the right to make that choice. That is what college and career readiness is all about. Even if a student elects to enter the world of work after high school, if he or she is to secure a job that will earn more than a minimum wage and have a career path that will lead to additional responsibility and a better salary, a sound academic high school education is key. This is why forty-five states have adopted the Common Core Standards grounded in rigorous expectations and world-class expectations (National Governors Association, 2010). The challenge now is to not affirm that all students can learn, which was a slogan of the past, but rather to affirm that all students can learn to read well, to write with clarity and confidence, to understand how to apply mathematical thinking, to think critically, to communicate in a second language, and to understand the principles of science. We are at a crossroads where we must choose whether all students develop the higher level skills and complex knowledge needed for this new century, or whether we continue to prepare only the lucky and the elite for success.

Can this be accomplished? Our experience and practice tell us that the answer to that question is *yes*. However, schools cannot realize that ideal with heavy-handed testing and punitive measures for teachers and schools. Students' life circumstances most certainly impact their learning—we do not subscribe to the "no excuses" philosophy that refuses to acknowledge the inequities in students' lives and in the funding for the schools they attend. Wise educators know that meaningful reform does not happen overnight and that it is complex.

That wisdom guided Finland as it transformed its educational system (Finnish National Board of Education, 2004). Social conditions must be addressed, structures must become equitable, curriculum must be revised, and instruction must change.

In this book, we address those factors that schools can control. We believe that there are four critical ingredients—acceleration, critical thinking, equitable practices, and support (ACES)—which, when deliberately interwoven into curriculum, instruction, and structure, work together to bring all students to college and career readiness. Although any of these four can have a positive impact on learning, when they are systematically combined, they create a synergy that can transform classrooms and schools.

The enriched curriculum and teaching strategies that promote critical thinking and college and career ready achievement for our most proficient students must be consistently used with all students. It is not just for those who come in the most prepared to learn. Although students surely will choose different paths when they leave us, it is our job to make sure that when they graduate they will be able to make a choice as to which path they will follow, and that they can be successful in the choice they make.

The solutions posed in this book are not for readers who want a quick, politically expedient solution. Rather, they are designed for those who are willing to persistently engage in deep change that emanates from the belief that all students can become college ready. We believe the tools and strategies that we present here are both timely and valuable. We hope you agree.

1 Becoming College and Career Ready

We have struggled to align student learning at the end of high school with the demands of college-level work, beginning with core areas such as mathematics and language arts . . . Clear learning goals for these fundamental skills through K–12 education will give students and teachers a better roadmap toward the goal of success in college and life.

Paul E. Lingenfelter, President,
State Higher Education Executive Officers

WHAT DOES IT MEAN TO BE COLLEGE AND CAREER READY?

Being college and career ready means that our students will leave our high schools with the knowledge and skills they need—whether they choose college, trade school, or a highly skilled job in the 21st century workplace. Although our students will vary in skill and ambition, all of them have the right to make the choice between college and career, and educators must give them what they need to make the best decision. Whichever path they choose, we know that in order to be successful, they must be confident, self-directed, and independent learners. College and career ready (CCR) is the new baseline.

If we are to effectively prepare our students, we must begin with a common understanding of what we mean when we say a student is ready for college and for career. In this book we use two contemporary, expert sources to guide our understanding of readiness. The first is a 2003 report titled, *Understanding University Success,* which summarized the findings of a three-year study sponsored by the Association of American Universities and the

Pew Charitable Trusts. Its purpose was to identify the skills and knowledge students need in order to be ready for the first year of college study.

Our second source is the Common Core State Standards (CCSS) created by educational experts and policymakers. These standards, which have been adopted in forty-two of our fifty states, communicate what students should learn in the K–12 grades in order to be prepared for the first year of college, postsecondary job training, or a highly skilled job that will earn more than a minimum wage (National Governors Association, 2010). Below we explain what both are about.

UNDERSTANDING UNIVERSITY SUCCESS AND THE KSUS STANDARDS

As noted above, the participants in *Understanding University Success* worked to make college-ready skills transparent to policy makers and educators. To that end, four hundred faculty members and college administrators from twenty prominent research universities engaged in extensive conversations which resulted in the identification of specific skills and content knowledge needed by students in order to be successful in first-year college courses. The report resulted in what are commonly referred to as the Knowledge and Skills for University Success (KSUS) standards (Conley, 2003).

KSUS participants created specific and comprehensive standards across the curricula designed to inform secondary schools of what students need to know and to be able to do to be successful during the critical first year of college. They hoped that by doing so, they would influence high school instruction, assessments, and curricula. The standards cover six areas of curriculum—English, mathematics, the natural sciences, the social sciences, world languages, and the arts. For each area, the faculty members identified foundational skills as well as specific content knowledge (Conley, 2003).

What can we learn from what the KSUS committee had to say? The identified habits of mind are listed below and, according to the KSUS standards, define the successful first-year college student:

- Inquisitive
- Willing to take risks, accept feedback, and learn from mistakes
- Skilled in critical and analytical thinking
- Able to draw inferences and reach conclusions based on the critical evaluation of sources
- Skilled in supporting their opinions with sound and coherent arguments

Across the six areas of curriculum, college professors identified these skills as needed for college success. The KSUS standards provide both general and specific examples. Whether they are standards for mathematics or for the arts, the habits of mind such as the habit of critical thinking listed above, are a common thread. In addition, there is clear overlap between KSUS and the College and Career Ready Standards (CCRS) of the Common Core, suggesting that the authors of the Common Core had the KSUS standards in mind when they developed the Common Core State Standards in English language arts and mathematics. You will recognize the similarities between the two as you read the next section.

THE COMMON CORE STATE STANDARDS

The Common Core State Standards (CCSS) are the second source we use to describe what it means to be college and career ready. Although they are more general than the KSUS standards, they are also more comprehensive in that they build from the elementary years to the end of high school study. The CCSS are K–12 standards, built with a backward design. The commencement standards were identified and then each standard was described at the various levels of schooling.

The CCSS were developed by the National Governors Association along with the Council of Chief State Superintendent Officers. The intent was to build a national consensus around what students need to be able to do in order to be ready for both college and the world of work. Policymakers realized that the proficiency standards, which were independently developed by states under No Child Left Behind (NCLB), resulted in unevenness in preparation across the nation (Porter, McMaken, Hwang, & Yang, 2011). Therefore, the authors of the CCSS designed them based upon what they believed to be the best state and international standards. They are similar to the KSUS standards in their emphasis on the development of critical thinking skills and a sound foundation in literacy and mathematics.

When we read the CCSS, we were surprised by how ambitious, in both breadth and rigor, they are. Their rigor is due, in part, to their incorporation of the KSUS expectations. As we read them, we were also struck by how similar the 12th grade learning outcomes are to the measured outcomes of the International Baccalaureate exams.

For example, higher level thinking is more prominent in the Common Core than in all present state standards (Porter et al., 2011). The standards for English language arts cannot be met in English classes alone. Literacy and critical thinking must be taught and practiced across the curricula if students are to meet the standards. The reading of informational texts is emphasized, and there are reading and writing standards for the sciences, social sciences, and technical subjects.

WHAT MUST SCHOOLS DO TO MAKE OUR STUDENTS COLLEGE AND CAREER READY?

The best way for educators to make sure that our students reach the identified high learning standards is by infusing them into our curriculum and instruction K–12. Although college and career may seem far off in the distance when considering an elementary-aged student, we know that if we wait until high school, it is too late. The practice of critical thinking, the skill of communicating with purpose and clarity, the knowledge of how to form well substantiated arguments, the competency in mathematical thinking that bring our students to fluency, accuracy and depth in mathematics, as well as the other skills identified in the KSUS and CCSS, need to be fostered and developed throughout school years.

This will not be an easy task. As enthusiastic as policymakers might be about the standards, educators understand how difficult this will be, especially at a time when school budgets are shrinking, not expanding. For some students who come from well-resourced homes, the standards will not be difficult to achieve. For our English language learners (ELLs), for our students who struggle with Standard English, and for our students with disabilities, the challenge will be much greater. If we do not move forward with their needs in mind, we fear that the standards will devolve into a mechanism to sort students into different life paths, using tests to indicate readiness. That is, the movement to ramp up expectations can quickly turn into another mechanism to sort, stratify, and decrease expectations for students who face the most daunting obstacles outside of school.

We believe that we must jealously guard the interests of our most vulnerable students as the CCSS are put in place. How schools can build the rigor and skill of college and career readiness K–12 for *all* students, then, is the purpose of this book in which we focus on *equitable excellence*. In the following chapters, we provide the theory, strategies, examples, and models for educators to use in order to help all students reach CCR goals. We share what we have learned from being part of a district team that has closed achievement gaps, moved the vast majority of students into International Baccalaureate courses, and increased the number of our graduates who complete college in four years (Burris & Garrity, 2009; Burris & Welner, 2005; Burris, Welner, Wiley, & Murphy, 2008; Garrity, 2004). If students are to truly be prepared for the challenges that await them, college and career readiness strategies cannot become systemic test prep activities. It must be about change in structure, curriculum, lessons, practice, and expectations.

THE FOUR INSTRUCTIONAL PRINCIPLES: ACES

Real reform takes both hard work and a willingness to change the status quo. We have learned from our experiences as well as from the research that guided us that there are four key instructional principles that can help the nation prepare all students for college and career readiness. These principles are what we refer to as the four **ACES**—**A**cceleration, **C**ritical thinking, **E**quitable practices, and **S**upport (**ACES**). When these four principles are used to inform curriculum, teaching, and instructional design features, such as grouping practices, students can acquire the skills that they need to be successful in postsecondary education. Each component of ACES will be discussed in its own chapter, along with the research and theory that supports it. In the final chapter we will provide sample lessons that are transformed to include principles of ACES so that they are infused with rigor and challenge.

Chapter 2 will focus on the principle of **acceleration**. Accelerated instruction is an alternative to traditional remediation, which results counterproductively in expanding learning gaps among students (Levin, 1988). Accelerated instruction is based on three key principles. The first principle is the maximal use of instructional time for each individual student in order to increase his or her learning. The second is spiraled curriculum that eliminates the need for redundancy, especially in mathematics. The final principle is the belief that the enriched curriculum designed for traditional gifted and talented students is the best curriculum for all. Chapter 2 explains how we can accelerate the learning of students through transfer (building on prior knowledge), compacted curriculum, enrichment, and simple teaching strategies that make the optimal use of instructional time. We include model lesson plans as well as teaching tips in the chapter.

Critical thinking, which the KSUS and CCSS standards have identified as necessary for college and career success, is at the heart of the rich curriculum that has been so successful in preparing our own students. The anchor standards of the Common Core include the language of higher level thinking sprinkled throughout. Students are expected to infer from text, evaluate arguments, and analyze documents. The development of such skills must begin long before the final years of high school. In Chapter 3 we will share strategies on how K–12 lessons can be transformed to ensure that students engage in higher level thinking.

The focus of Chapter 3 is the skillful use of Bloom's Taxonomy to promote **critical thinking**. We use the revised version which focuses on level of complexity and knowledge type (Anderson & Krathwohl, 2001). Chapter 3 includes a guide for lesson planning as well as an example of how to analyze a lesson based on the taxonomy. As we do in Chapter 2, we again include sample lessons as well as questions for discussion.

For some students, the development of CCR skills will take place as part of the natural flow of learning. Other students will need more help. Some students have parents who will be strong advocates of college preparatory experiences while other students rely on professional educators to be their advocates. Providing access to challenging learning is at the very heart of what it is means to be an **equitable** school that meets the needs of all of its students. So often the very strategies that we use with our most vulnerable learners—remediation and drill—exacerbate learning gaps instead of closing them (Burris & Garrity, 2008; Levin, 1988; Oakes, 2005), thus pushing further and further away the goal of being ready for success beyond high school. Chapter 4 will provide the strategies needed to avoid ineffective grouping practices in order to create classrooms in which instruction, not standards, are differentiated for learners. Chapter 4 also includes a description of how to differentiate instruction while maintaining high learning standards for all members of the class. It provides sample lessons at the elementary, middle, and high school level.

This leads us naturally to our fourth principle—**support**—which is the focus of Chapter 5. There we explain how to create effective supports for learners who struggle, providing access to the same accelerated and enriched experiences that will give them the confidence and skills needed to be college and career ready. The model that we propose and develop is one in which support, whether it be in the mainstream class, support class, ELL class, or resource room, is characterized by relevance and rigor. Providing Response to Intervention (RTI) services is discussed in this chapter, and like prior chapters, we include sample lessons designed to show how to support struggling learners in both the mainstream and support classroom.

Chapter 6 provides models of how the four principles can be used synergistically to create classrooms that promote CCR standards in a way in which all students can be both supported and challenged. By showing how to integrate practices associated with each of the ACES, we provide a method by which educators can examine their present practices and transform them. In this chapter, we offer lessons that are designed to integrate the four principles that guide this book and to meet the expectations of the Common Core standards. Those lessons show how ACES can be integrated. The chapter concludes with advice on how teachers can analyze and level up their own lessons.

In all chapters, we provide practical K–12 curricular perspectives, instructional strategies, and lesson plans that provide examples of how to implement acceleration, critical thinking, equity, and support in lessons. In order to help the reader understand why each sample lesson was included, we connect the sample lessons to the KSUS standards and the CCSS. This integration of the book's content with the CCSS is intended to deepen the reader's understanding of the standards and how they can be realized in classroom K–12 lessons in a way that invites all students to learn in a challenged, meaningful way. By providing these linked examples, we intend to spark the creativity of our readers so that they can successfully create new strategies and lessons of their own to help their students become college and career ready. The integration of the Common Core State Standards will take thought and planning as teachers juggle all of the competing demands that they must meet each day—our hope is that this book will be of assistance in this endeavor. We now begin with our first principle—Acceleration.

2 Accelerated Instruction for All Learners— The *A* in ACES

THE EFFECT OF TIME ON INSTRUCTION

A friend once recounted a conversation he heard while serving on an advisory board of a research council. During a discussion of the effects of extended time on testing, someone asked if time really mattered in test taking? A colleague, whose expertise was in physics, replied that it did— only in the *real* world.

Time certainly matters in our *real* world of education! We teach and our students learn within the constraints of time. When we were classroom teachers, we often felt as if time were the enemy—if only there were one more day to spend on a unit, or if only the period were an hour instead of just forty-five minutes. We always thought about how much we could do if only we had more time for our students who were struggling.

Ironically, for our struggling learners, we often ineffectively use the time we do have as we frantically try to catch them up with repetitive drills and more worksheets. As a result, rather than catching up, students fall even further behind. And so the achievement gap as well as the expectation gap widens. As a result, these students can never be college and career ready because they do not learn the critical thinking skills, the content, and the strategies they need for learning after high school.

One of the first educators to recognize the primacy of time in learning was the great educational psychologist Benjamin Bloom (1913–1999). Bloom is best remembered for the taxonomy of educational objectives known as Bloom's Taxonomy of the Cognitive Domain. This taxonomy helps us understand the complexity of thinking, especially higher level thinking, and will be the focus of the following chapter. In addition to the taxonomy, however, Dr. Bloom also developed the idea of mastery learning. He believed that 95 percent of all students could learn each subject to high levels of mastery provided they are given enough time and the optimal learning situation designed for them. According to Bloom, both opportunity and effort play a critical role in student learning (Bloom, 1968).

Bloom advocated change in the delivery of instruction. In many ways, Bloom championed differentiated instruction long before the term was coined. He was an advocate of peer support groups, cooperative learning, one on one tutorials, the use of technology, and different texts and materials for different students. While recognizing that some students need more time, he was more interested in how educators could *reduce* the time struggling students needed to learn by changing strategies to more effectively deliver instruction. Schools, he believed, were responsible for creating the conditions to accelerate learning, not holding it back (Bloom, 1968).

Mastery Learning and Remediation

Unfortunately, mastery learning's advocates over-emphasized the sequential nature of learning, and they insisted that students not move on until each skill was mastered. This idea gave rise to remedial strategies and low-track classes. In the 1970s, coauthor Garrity's school used an instructional mastery model of individualized learning in mathematics which could be best described as *seats and sheets*. Initially, a teacher taught a mini lesson on a given topic and distributed worksheets for independent practice. As students satisfactorily completed the worksheet, they would move on to a new topic via a new mini lesson and a new sheet, thus theoretically progressing through the curriculum at their own pace. Instructional and curricular issues arose, however, when some students moved ahead to another topic or grade level, while other students, who did not demonstrate topic mastery, were required to keep practicing by completing more sheets.

Thus in the name of mastery, wide learning and achievement gaps developed. Teachers became frustrated by their inability to *teach* a lesson, and the math class was transformed into a factory of students sitting in seats attempting to master sheets. In time, the model gave way to tracked math classes. The students in the low track fell further behind, believing that they could not do math and that they were not good enough for a challenging education. This example illustrates why traditional remediation does not work.

The Problem With Traditional Remediation

Research into the effects of remediation demonstrates the ineffectiveness of the practice. John M. Peterson (1989), a professor of mathematics at Brigham Young University, conducted a research study in three similar Utah school districts. He compared the effects of different junior high math programs on students identified as remedial, average, or accelerated. He describes the results of that study in a 1989 article titled "Remediation is No Remedy."

In that study, seventh-grade remedial students were divided into three groups and placed into either a remedial class, a class with average curriculum moving at a slower pace, or a heterogeneously grouped accelerated prealgebra course. The remedial students who were placed in the accelerated prealgebra class showed significant improvement in math skills as compared with the remedial students in either the remedial program or the regular seventh-grade curriculum. Peterson (1989) concluded that remedial students learn more in programs designed to accelerate learning than in slower paced programs designed to remediate their math skills.

Peterson was not alone in his findings. Kifer, Wolfe, and Schmidt (1993) demonstrated almost no growth for students placed in remedial eighth-grade classrooms. A study by White, Gamoran, Porter, and Smithson (1996) gives additional support for accelerating the learning of math of low-achieving students, rather than placing them in a low-track class with a curriculum of remediation. In their study, students who were "misplaced" into higher-track classes did better than students in the low-track classes in which they should have been assigned. In summary, the idea that students should continue to be drilled on basic skills before moving on results in a deleterious effect on their learning.

There is another, more effective approach we can use if we are committed to prepare all of our students, not just an elite group of students, for college and career. We have learned from both research and our own practice that a better course of action is to accelerate rather than decelerate student learning.

The concept of accelerated instruction was first proposed in the 1980s by Hank Levin, then of Stanford University, now of Teachers College, Columbia University. Accelerated instruction is not about racing through the curriculum. Rather, it is about the maximal use of instructional time for each individual student in order to accelerate learning. While recognizing the differences among learners, the accelerated model is founded on the belief that the instructional model designed for the most talented students is the best model for all (Burris, Heubert, & Levin, 2006; Burris & Garrity, 2009; Levin, 1988). Accelerated instructional strategies do not ignore the differences among learners, rather they incorporate supplementary strategies and work through those differences.

The principles that guide accelerated instruction are quite different from those on which remediation is founded. Enrichment combined with higher level thinking is a hallmark of the accelerated classroom. Advocates of the accelerated approach believe that all students can benefit from the approaches used in classrooms for the gifted and talented (Finnan, St. John, Mc Carthy, & Slovacek, 1996). Accelerated lessons are designed to capture student interest, with minimal reliance on worksheets and repetition. Rather than slowing down instruction until each skill is mastered, skills are revisited in later lessons (spiraling) or buttressed in resource rooms, ELL classes, or support classes that are designed to support mainstream lessons. Formative assessments of student learning allow the teacher to know how to develop instruction during the unit. If needed, instructional time is added outside of the school day. Figure 2.1 summarizes the difference between traditional remedial instruction and accelerated instruction.

As Jeff Zweirs (2008) explains in his book, *Building Academic Language*, "they [students who underperform] need rich classroom experiences that accelerate the language that supports their content knowledge, thinking skills, and literacy skills...and they need accelerated learning because their high-performing peers do not just linger around, waiting for them to catch up" (p. xiv).

Accelerated instruction is inclusive instruction. All students are in classrooms that teach enriched curriculum. Compacting of curriculum takes places whenever possible—either whole class or individualized in differentiated lessons or units of study. Pre-assessment and spiraled review are important tools to guide and reinforce instruction.

The philosophy of accelerated schooling is embodied in the Accelerated Schools Project, which has been in existence for several decades (Levin, 1987). Evaluations of accelerated programs have demonstrated gains in student achievement, including the achievement of low achieving students (Bloom, Ham, Melton, & O'Brient, 2001; Burris et al., 2006; Finnan & Swanson, 2000). In the following sections, we share examples of how strategies that accelerate instruction can be used K–12 in classrooms.

Great teachers have so much in common. Their lessons have clear learning objectives that are known by their students. They are well prepared for each class they teach. The materials that they use complement

Figure 2.1 Characteristics of Remedial Instruction and Accelerated Instruction

Remedial Instruction	Accelerated Instruction
Students are pulled out of the mainstream classroom for remediation or assigned to remedial or low-track classes for instruction	Support services are push-in services or take place outside mainstream instructional time in support classes. Students are included in the mainstream classroom.
Instruction is skill based.	Instruction integrates the teaching of skills within an enriched curriculum. Features of gifted instruction are incorporated into the lesson.
Instruction is sequential.	Instruction is spiraled, using transfer to accelerate learning. Concepts are reintroduced as needed.
Instruction relies on "more time on task" as the strategy for learning.	Instruction continues to advance while developing tools to address weaknesses in learning.
Building of skill is the curriculum.	Compensatory strategies are taught within the context of the curriculum.
Instruction relies primarily on individual seatwork.	Instruction regularly uses cooperative learning.
Instruction is direct and teacher centered.	Instruction is often constructivist and is student centered.
Goal is proficiency.	Goal is preparation for postsecondary learning.
Assessment is used to separate students and modify their curriculum.	Assessment is used to adjust and differentiate instruction or to provide support.
Student error is used to slow down instruction.	Student error is anticipated and the *Why* of common error is made transparent to students.

their instruction. They exude acceptance of their students and a deep concern for student learning. They are reflective—both inside and outside of the classroom.

Certainly all of the above characteristics of good teaching accelerate the learning of students—regardless of student demographics or school philosophy. There are other strategies, however, which when regularly implemented, can accelerate student learning. In this chapter, we will discuss four acceleration strategies in depth—transfer, assessment, compacting, and enrichment.

ACCELERATING LEARNING THROUGH TRANSFER

> Successful students are able to integrate personal experiences and knowledge with the material they encounter in their coursework. Information comes from a variety of sources whether it is from a different class or department, personal observation or public knowledge, students should be able to connect ideas and concepts across sources.
>
> *Understanding University Success*, p. 20

Our goal as educators is to teach for the transfer of knowledge. We do not want students to learn a list of Spanish vocabulary words for the sake of knowing the list. Our hope is that they will transfer that knowledge as they communicate in the language. We do not expect that our students will remember how to prove the sides of a triangle equal when they are forty years old. We want them to learn how to logically approach a problem when we teach them a geometric proof. When students in primary grades create a class birthday graph, not only does it serve as a visual reminder of birthday celebrations, but also the graph serves as a means by which teachers gently introduce mathematical concepts in order to provide a foundation for numeracy. The Common Core State Standards (CCSS) are built from a K–12 perspective, with each standard incorporating and building upon prior knowledge from earlier grade levels.

In addition to being a goal of education, transfer is also a principle of learning. Transfer of learning is the conscious or unconscious application of old learning to new. It occurs whether we want it to or not. Sometimes it is a help (positive transfer) and sometimes it is a hindrance (negative transfer). If we are aware of its existence and its potential, we can skillfully use it to accelerate instruction.

Positive Transfer

Positive transfer of what is known to what is new can be used to accelerate the learning of our students. For example, when a teacher helps a student make the connection between a word in an ELL student's first language to a word in English, that is an example of positive transfer. Likewise, foreign language teachers can make connections between the words in the second language and English to teach sophisticated English words (think *edificio* in Spanish and the English word, *edifice*). In order to use positive transfer to accelerate new learning, consider the following questions:

- What do students know (process, model, technique) that is similar to what they are to learn? What are the features of prior learning that are similar? What are the features that are dissimilar?

Negative Transfer

When students learn to phonetically deconstruct the words *distaste, implicate,* and *decide,* and they are then able to independently sound out *replicate,* positive transfer has occurred. However, when the same strategies are later used to sound out *epitome,* error occurs. That is an example of negative transfer. Negative transfer can cause students confusion when they impose rules or models that they have internalized to a new situation in which those rules or models do not apply. The ability to anticipate student error and to provide instruction that addresses error before it occurs is an important but often overlooked strategy to accelerate student learning. Negative transfer often impedes our students' learning. If a teacher is proactive, she can mitigate its effects.

In order to guard against negative transfer, ask the following questions:

- What do students already know that might interfere with the new learning?
- Is there a prior model that might interfere with the new understanding or knowledge?

After you have answered the above, devise a plan to thwart negative transfer. Make it known to students that what they are learning is different from what they have learned before. Explain how it is different and why a different strategy or model is appropriate for the learning at hand. By doing so, you will save valuable instructional time that would be spent on correcting error.

Coupling the transfer of knowledge from material that is of high interest to students can also be a powerful tool for teachers! The following lesson illustrates how transfer can be deliberately used to teach struggling students how to use a note-taking skill known as Cornell notes.

Model Lesson: Using Transfer to Introduce Cornell Note Taking

To be useful, a set of notes should be more than just a transcript of what a professor has said…Students are expected to pay close attention and engage with presented materials, both written and verbal. This requires taking in information, analyzing it and recording that which is meaningful and useful.

Understanding University Success, p. 18

Introduce a topic and organize ideas, concepts, and information to make important connections and distinctions; include formatting (e.g., headings), graphics (e.g., figures, tables), and multimedia when useful to aiding comprehension.

National Governors Association,
CCSS Writing Standards for Literacy, p. 65

If our goal is to prepare students for postsecondary education, note-taking skills are a must. With this in mind, we decided to teach our students how to use an established method of taking notes, Cornell notes. The advantage of Cornell notes is that they force students to categorize knowledge and process it by creating summary statements. The following lesson, designed for a special education support class, will focus on the use of transfer to help students understand how to effectively implement and apply note-taking skills.

The majority of the students in the class were boys who were very interested in baseball. The teacher decided to use a baseball scorecard as an example of a note-taking strategy that would be familiar to many students and would also be of high interest to the class. She recognized that a baseball scorecard has many features that are similar to the Cornell note sheet, and therefore could be used as a powerful tool for transfer of prior knowledge. Both the scorecard and the note-taking sheet provide detailed information on the right-hand side of the sheet. On the left-hand side of both there are labels. For Cornell notes, these labels are topics. For a baseball scorecard, the label is the name of the player who is up at bat. On the bottom of both a baseball scorecard and Cornell notes there is a space for summary.

The teacher began the lesson by asking the class how many had ever kept score at a baseball game. Several of the students had. The teacher showed the class a completed scorecard and allowed the students who were familiar with scorekeeping to explain its features to the class. She also allowed them to tell the class, using the scorecard, what had occurred during the fifth inning when a particular player was up at bat. The class was intrigued by the detail given by the abbreviations, and the student presenters were pleased and proud to share their knowledge. Pointing to the bottom of the scorecard, the teacher asked the students to summarize how well the pitcher did based on the hits and runs he gave up.

The teacher then told the class that they were going to learn a note-taking technique, called Cornell notes, that was very similar to keeping a baseball scorecard, and, if they learned to use it well, they would find it to be as good a source of information on what happened in class as a baseball scorecard is a great source of information about what happened at a ballgame. The teacher explained the three sections of the Cornell note-taking sheet and had the students make connections between each section and the baseball scorecard.

After modeling how to take Cornell notes, the teacher gave each student a short article on acid rain, a topic that they were studying in biology. There were five different articles on the topic, which varied by reading level. The students independently read their article, paired up with another student who had the same article, and put notes on what they read on the right-hand side of the Cornell note-taking sheet. They then created topic labels on the left-hand side, and after some modeling by the teacher, the students wrote a three-sentence summary of the article in the summary section.

The teacher ended the class by asking students how Cornell notes were different from baseball scorecards. Students shared that with baseball scorecards, the labels (names of the players) were known before the notes were taken. They also noted that on a scorecard notes were taken in columns, but on the new note-taking sheet the notes were written across the entire note-taking area. Finally, they noted that with Cornell notes, they were responsible for creating the topical sections, but on a scorecard, the sections were determined based on who was at bat. The teacher also asked the class how this technique differs from how they previously took notes. The class listed the advantages of the new strategy when compared with old practices.

The following day, students used their notes to share with the class what their article was about. The class also discussed why they chose

(Continued)

(Continued)

the labels for each note-taking section. Later, when their biology class studied acid rain, students would transfer the knowledge that they learned in the note-taking lesson (Figure 2.2).

Figure 2.2 Cornell Notes

Name: Joe Torres	Class: Biology	Date: 4/2/11
Aim: What is acid rain?		

Topics or questions	Supporting details
Description	Rain that is acidic. The PH is low (0-4). Snow, sleet, and ice can have acid.
Cause of acid rain	Caused by man-made pollution. Ex- sulfur dioxide and nitrogen oxide. Chemicals in the air from burning fossil fuel ex.. Coal and from car emission
Problems	Can kill trees in the forests, pollute lakes & streams. Pollution in the water—kills fish, frogs, salamanders. Bad for food chain! makes paint peel. destroys statues and monuments
Solutions	EPA laws on pollution, cars with low emission, less dependence On fossil fuels. Go green!

Summary

Acid rain is a serious issue in the environment. It hurts our food chain, our forests and our world. It should be monitored and we should reduce our use of fossil fuels.

Reflection on the Lesson

The teacher facilitated the transfer of student understanding of a known model, specifically a baseball scorecard to a new model, the Cornell note-taking sheet. The scorecard incorporated all of the features of the model she wanted to teach. In addition, it introduced the idea of using symbols and abbreviations to take notes, something she would come back to during a later lesson. The scorecard was of high interest to the class and quickly captured student interest. The lesson was student-centered—students explained the baseball scorecard to the class, noted the similar features, independently practiced, and the next day taught the class about acid rain using their notes.

Practice materials were related to the content area, the study of acid rain. She could have chosen articles on baseball or other sports, but a feature of accelerated instruction is that the teaching of skills does not occur in isolation but rather within the context of curriculum. Baseball was used to expedite learning, but the class then quickly returned to curriculum that was being learned in the mainstream class to practice the skill.

During the lesson, the teacher was cognizant that negative transfer could occur. For nearly all students, taking notes is an unwelcome chore. They are never sure what to write down and often write too little or too much. Student notes, especially those of the least proficient students, tend to be disorganized lists. Therefore, it is important that students do not transfer old note-taking behaviors to the new format. Without our diligent awareness of the possibility of negative transfer, students will simply replicate the same ineffective procedures. To prevent negative transfer, the teacher made it transparent to the students how Cornell notes differed from both a scorecard and from other note-taking strategies that they had used in the past. She anticipated what could interfere with good note-taking practices. By including a pair activity and an oral presentation, she incorporated CCSS for speaking and listening into the lesson.

ACCELERATING LEARNING THROUGH ASSESSMENT

During the summer, our high school had an opening for a mathematics teacher. Several good candidates taught demonstration lessons in our summer program. The students who were in the geometry summer class were those who had failed the Regents exam in June and were preparing to retake it.

Each of the candidates was given a topic to teach. Three of the candidates taught the topic from the very beginning, as though students had never been taught the topic before. One candidate did not. He assumed prior knowledge and began with carefully crafted questions that allowed him to find out what the students knew. It was apparent that they knew a lot more than the other candidates had assumed! He developed the lesson grounded in their complete (and sometimes incomplete) knowledge. He carefully adjusted instruction when he encountered gaps in understanding. He provided cues to help students remember. He was the only candidate who was able to complete the topic so that students were confident by the end of class. The other candidates rushed through the lesson, and it was not known whether students understood the lesson or not. It takes confidence to teach as the successful math candidate did—confidence in your own knowledge of content, and perhaps more importantly, confidence in students. He did not assume that because these students were in summer school they did not know anything about geometry. Students know when a teacher holds high expectations for them—they feel dignified and challenged, and they respond.

Teachers who accelerate student learning *teach up* to their students. They do not get bogged down in multiple examples or extensive homework reviews. If they notice that some students are not grasping content, they do not repeat what they have said, rather they say it a different way. They constantly assess learning and use that assessment to monitor and adjust instruction. Formal assessments as well as informal assessments can also provide valuable information to accelerate learning. By analyzing the errors that students made on the New York State Global History and Geography examination, our teachers realized that students often made errors, not due to a lack of knowledge of history, but due to a lack of academic vocabulary. Deliberately including the development of vocabulary is now part of social studies lessons. It is also in keeping with the college and career readiness standard for vocabulary acquisition and use across the curriculum.

ACCELERATING LEARNING THROUGH COMPACTING CURRICULUM

> Some students may decide at any early age that they want to take Calculus or other college level courses in high school. These students would need to begin the study of high school content in the middle school, which would lead to Precalculus or Advanced Statistics as a junior and Calculus, Advanced Statistics or other college level options as a senior.
>
> National Governors Association,
> CCSS for Mathematics, Appendix A, p. 3

> Entering students need to know basic mathematical concepts—computation, algebra, trigonometry, geometry—so that they have the tools to work with increasingly complex conceptual mathematical and quantitative procedures and analyses in their college courses.
>
> *Understanding University Success*, p. 29

The best predictor of whether or not a student will complete college is whether they complete a math course at the level of trigonometry or above. Researcher Cliff Adelman (1999), in his study entitled *Answers in the*

Tool Box: Academic Intensity, Attendance Patterns, and Bachelor's Degree Attainment, analyzed years worth of longitudinal data to isolate those factors that are most related to whether a student finishes college. He looked at three factors which he called "academic resources"—test scores, class rank/GPA, and curriculum. What he found was that what we teach students matters—*curriculum contributed 41 percent to college completion, as compared with 30 percent for test scores, and 29 percent for class rank/GPA.* Adelman had the most to say about the importance of math. He found that the highest level of math a student studied was the most important factor of all. Enrollment in math beyond Algebra 2 (trigonometry and beyond) in high school "more than doubles the odds" of a student enrolled in college of actually completing a bachelor's degree (p. 3). It was a more powerful indicator of successful college completion than socioeconomic status. That is why we believe that it is important to get all students to algebra by Grade 8. This gives students the time that they need in high school to take the courses that are so important for college success, courses at the level of trigonometry and beyond (Adelman, 1999).

Compacting to Accelerate All Students in Mathematics

Acceleration of curriculum through compacting is a powerful way to increase learning. Using that technique, we were able to bring all students to algebra in Grade 8 so that more students, especially more of our disadvantaged students, could take the high level math courses needed for college success. What follows is a summary of how that was done and what was accomplished.

Teachers of mathematics at all grades, with the exception of K–2, engage in continual reteaching of prior skills although their curriculum mandates the extension or application of the skill. Rather than advancing instruction on the topic, teachers expand curriculum by reintroducing prior topics before teaching the new topic.

This same repetition frequently occurs during homework reviews. If the homework review is too lengthy, the teacher lacks the time to develop the daily topic, and as a consequence, students are confused and error must be corrected the following day—during homework review! This repetitive pattern of instruction results in an extraordinary waste of instructional time and in student boredom. By sixth grade, students who can catch on quickly become bored with repetitive topics. They learn math as a set of procedures to be memorized.

Students with less talent in mathematics never have the opportunity to develop the deep understanding that results when topics are properly developed. What they learn they quickly forget. In an attempt to address the learning gap, most schools begin to sort and select students for various tracks in mathematics, thus denying groups of students the opportunity to study advanced mathematics at the high school level. They consign those students to an even slower paced and more repetitive curriculum. As previously noted in the CCSS in mathematics, the only path to advanced coursework in high school mathematics is with the study of high school mathematics, specifically algebra, in the middle school. Once the academic door shuts in the middle school, it is virtually impossible for a student to open the door to advanced study at a later grade. The curriculum gap, and with it the achievement gap, become a wide chasm that is impossible to cross.

Accelerated instruction is a viable solution that affords all students the opportunity to learn mathematics in a heterogeneous classroom environment by studying an enriched challenging curriculum. Based on our district's belief that all middle school students would benefit from instruction in high level, heterogeneously grouped classes, we developed a multiyear plan to eliminate all tracking in math. We began with a careful review of the mathematics curriculum. Our middle school teachers came to the conclusion, that because of the repetition of topics, it would be possible to compact the curricula for Grades 6–8 into Grades 6–7, and teach the New York State algebra course to all students in Grade 8. In order to help all students be successful, the district added every-other-day support classes for any student who needed more instruction.

In June of 1998, the first cohort of detracked, accelerated students took the New York State Sequential I Regents examination in Grade 8. The middle school passing rate on the Sequential I Mathematics Regents exam proved to be higher than the district passing rate when students took the course in tracked middle and high school classes. Over 84 percent passed the exam, and 52 percent were at the mastery level with a score of 85 percent or above. That passing rate on the exam continued to improve, and now is well over 90 percent each year.

Prior to accelerating all students in mathematics, no more than 23 percent of the senior class studied AP calculus in Grade 12. Today after thirteen years in which all students accelerate in mathematics starting in Grade 5, nearly 90 percent of all graduates pass a New York State Regents advanced mathematics course in advanced algebra and trigonometry. More than 70 percent pass an International Baccalaureate course in mathematics or AP calculus. The students who benefited the most from acceleration were the district's Latino and black students.

For our minority students, universal acceleration more than tripled the percentage of students who studied calculus. The yearly rate increased from 11 percent to as high as 50 percent after all students were accelerated.

Nearly 70 percent of all minority students take and pass a state exam in advanced algebra and trigonometry prior to high school graduation. At the same time, the policy of accelerating all did not depress the scores of high achieving students.

Although the details on this acceleration reform are beyond the scope of this book, two journal articles provide more information on the reform process as well as the findings based on a longitudinal study of this reform (Burris, Heubert, & Levin, 2004; Burris et al., 2006). We illustrate how math topics can be compacted to promote acceleration with the following example.

Compacting the Teaching of Fractions

According to the CCSS, the conceptual understanding of what a fraction is, along with computational operations with fractions, should be taught during Grades 3–7. Adding and subtracting fractions with like denominators and multiplying a fraction by a whole number begin in Grade 4 along with the introduction of equivalent fractions. However, the adding and subtracting with unlike denominators will not be taught until Grade 5. In Grade 5, teachers will reteach the operations with like denominators, expand to unlike denominators, and include multiplication of fractions and the concept of a fraction as division. Teachers in Grade 6 who must "finish" division of fractions feel compelled to reteach all operations of fractions based on the assumption that more time on task will yield mastery. If the complete reteaching of each fractional topic was eliminated however, fractions as a unit of study could be completed by the end of Grade 5.

With fractions, as with any mathematical concept, the most effective instructional approach is to develop a unit of study with lessons that incorporate concrete and visual representations of the concept along with the use of manipulatives. These instructional strategies help students develop deep understanding and then build to the general rule or algorithm. When computational skills are developed in this manner, followed by an appropriate amount of initial practice, understanding deepens (Thompson, 2009). If it is then reinforced with spiral review and assessment throughout the year, retention increases as well. In addition, positive transfer occurs as the student connects the visual model to the abstract arithmetic algorithm.

In contrast, when a teacher approaches computation as a procedural—*this is how you do it, now do it*—the students do not have that prior experiential knowledge upon which to build their knowledge and retention is diminished. The probability of negative transfer occurring increases as students try to guess the proper procedure from rote memorization. In

Chapter 4 on equity, we will return to the topic of how to provide initial instruction that results in deeper understanding with a lesson extension that introduces the concept of and operations with fractions using living graphs. The lesson below, however, illustrates how mathematics instruction can be compacted and accelerated while accommodating for student differences.

Model Lesson: Developing Division of Fractions—Grade 5

Mathematically proficient students look closely to discern a pattern or structure.

National Governors Association,
CCSS for Mathematics, p. 8

Students use the meaning of fractions, the meanings of multiplication and division, and the relationship between multiplication and division to understand and explain why the procedures for dividing fractions make sense.

National Governors Association,
CCSS for Mathematics, p. 39

Problem-solving involves analytical processes and sets of skills...successful students understand the relationships that exist between mathematical concepts and that formulas do not function in a vacuum. They perceive mathematics as a way of understanding, a thinking process and not a collection of detached procedures to be learned and apply separately.

Understanding University Success, p. 29

This series of lessons uses visuals and fraction tiles to demonstrate and develop division of rational numbers leading to the algorithm of using the reciprocal. Each component of the lesson is designed to relate division to multiplication and to help students understand that division by a proper fraction results in a larger number. These lessons were taught in a heterogeneously grouped fifth-grade class that included special education, ELL, and Standard English learners (SEL). A special education teacher assistant provided additional support to students.

The teacher began with a Do Now activity. A Do Now is a class warm up that sets the stage for a lesson. It often transfers old learning to new. In this lesson, the teacher used a practical problem to review the concept of division.

Day 1:

The Do Now:

Charlie is buying bags of chips for a picnic. At Debono's Deli a small bag cost $.50. At the local grocery store a small bag is $.75. (1) If Charlie has $6.00 to spend, how many bags can he get at each store? (2) Which store has the better deal? Draw an illustration to solve the problem.

Students initially worked independently and then discussed their solution with a partner. Partners drew an illustration of their solution. The teacher asked one pair to draw their solution for Debono's Deli and a second pair to draw their solution for the grocery store on chart paper. The pictures showed the dollars divided into ½s and ¾s, thus introducing division by ½ and ¾. The pictures were displayed on the board for future reference. The problem allowed students to use their prior knowledge of money to develop their understanding of dividing by a fraction.

The teacher then distributed a series of word problems using the unit fraction as a divisor. For each situation, the students would mark the picture to show the required length and then write a division sentence.

The first problem and visual model on their worksheet was this:

Jane is making blocks for her brother's kindergarten class. She purchases a board that is three feet long from which she will make the blocks. She has been asked to make the blocks half a foot in length.

Division Sentence	Answer

(Continued)

(Continued)

The teacher asked for a volunteer to read the problem aloud and then asked, "What kind of problem do we have here and how do you know?" After an appropriate amount of think time, the class indicated that it was a division problem and explained why. She asked students to make the marks on the paper for making the half-foot blocks and write their division sentence. The teacher and teacher assistant circulated to offer assistance as needed. After completing the first problem, students shared their results with a partner. One pair of students recorded their work on a piece of chart paper and shared it with the class. Using the student's visual of the problem and the division sentence, the teacher reinforced the concept of division by emphasizing the question and counting each part.

Division Sentence	Answer
$3 \div \dfrac{1}{2}$	6

She said, "How many $\dfrac{1}{2}$s are there in 3? Let's count them from the picture."

The second and third problems followed the same pattern using a board three feet in length. Now Jane has to make blocks one-third of a foot and one-fourth of a foot in length. As students worked independently, the teacher and special education assistant monitored student work. Students shared their results with a partner. Pairs volunteered their solutions.

The teacher again asked, "How many $\dfrac{1}{3}$s are there in 3? Let's count them from the picture." And again following the pattern, "How many $\dfrac{1}{4}$s are there in 3? Let's count them from the picture."

Division Sentence	Answer
$3 \div \dfrac{1}{4}$	12

The students moved to the fourth problem that posed the situation of creating blocks that were three-fourths of a foot from a board three feet in length. Again students solved this pictorially, wrote a division sentence, and then shared the answer with a partner. The teacher used the same structure to review this problem. The class discussed why 12, which is a common but incorrect answer, is not the answer when dividing 3 by $\dfrac{3}{4}$. When she was sure that students understood, she assigned homework. She posed the question: "Do you see a pattern for dividing fractions using multiplication?" For the special education, ELL, and SEL students, the classroom teacher created an additional visual reference sheet to scaffold this assignment. The paper included the visual representation of $4 \div \dfrac{1}{2}, 4 \div \dfrac{1}{3}, 4 \div \dfrac{1}{4},$ and $4 \div \dfrac{2}{3}$.

Day 2:

The Do Now revisited the blocks that Jane is making for the kindergarten class using a whole number divided by a unit fraction and a non-unit fraction. The teacher planned to use this to transition into the homework assignment review.

In solving these problems, draw a picture and write a division sentence.

The kindergarten class needed smaller pieces, so Jane used a three-foot board and divided it into pieces one-sixth of a foot in length. How many pieces did she have? How many pieces can she make if each block is two-sixths of a foot in length?

A possible pattern for using multiplication to solve division of fraction problems began to emerge. The students shared with a partner their

(Continued)

(Continued)

response to the previous day's homework assignment, "Do you see a pattern for dividing fractions using multiplication?" The students discovered the relationship between multiplying fractions and dividing fractions as multiplying by the reciprocal. They did not know the term *reciprocal* but certainly understood its function. The vocabulary word was naturally introduced. The teacher engaged the students in the use of the new vocabulary word, *reciprocal*. The teacher demonstrated the reciprocal in the context of the Do Now examples and asked the students to orally repeat the word after her three times. With a partner, each student orally described how to use a reciprocal when dividing fractions. Selected pairs shared their description.

On Day 2, the students tested more variations. For example, what would happen if a fraction was divided by a fraction? The teacher used fraction tiles to explore this question. Students worked in pairs with the fraction tiles using a series of examples starting with a fraction divided by a unit fraction, $\frac{1}{3}$ divided by $\frac{1}{6}$. The class progressed to $\frac{10}{12}$ divided by $\frac{5}{12}$, $\frac{2}{3}$ divided by $\frac{1}{12}$, and $\frac{2}{3}$ divided by $\frac{2}{12}$. For each example, the students sketched the solution from the tiles. The teacher allowed plenty of time for more exploration and pattern discovery. The students discovered the relationship between multiplying fractions and dividing fractions as multiplying by the reciprocal. To build academic vocabulary, the teacher emphasized the new vocabulary word in each example. She assigned the homework—four fraction problems. Students had to explain each solution in words or with a visual. If needed, students were permitted to take a set of fraction tiles home.

Day 3:

The Do Now included three fraction examples from the prior lessons. Students had the option of using fraction tiles. Explanations for solutions were required either using a picture or the reciprocal.

Day 3 introduced mixed numbers via practical situations—again with visuals—looking for patterns and testing the reciprocal.

The new problem was this:

The town has decided to build a playing field for children to play soccer and softball. The field measures 2 ½ acres. Each bag of grass seed will seed ¾ of an acre. Using your knowledge of division, how many bags of grass seed are required to seed the field? Will there be any seed left over to reseed parts of the field that may become worn due to over use?

Given a sheet with five word problems similar to the one above, students worked in small, heterogeneous groups to solve one of the five problems. The teacher balanced the groups to include students with academic needs along with highly proficient students. The students then regrouped in a jigsaw model to share the solution to the given problem with the other groups. Each student was responsible for completing all problems.

They were given a homework assignment:

Complete a "Write About" (see Figure 2.3) that includes five vocabulary words and one fraction problem to solve with numbers and then describe in words using the proper vocabulary.

Figure 2.3 Write About: How I Divide Fractions

Use this problem	Key words used in this topic
$\dfrac{2}{3} \div \dfrac{1}{6}$	Fraction
	Reciprocal
	Multiply
	Divide
	Simplify

TRY A MUSICAL APPLICATION! A new electric guitar is on sale for $240. What is the original price of the guitar if the sale sign reads ¼ off?

Reflection on the Lesson

In the initial Do Now, the teacher used the students' prior knowledge of money as a means to transfer learning to the new topic of division of fractions. The two questions represented two levels of complexity—the first requires application, the second simply requires recognition that .50 is less than .75. The use of .50 and .75 reflected two levels of difficulty—manipulating .5 is far less intimidating than working with .75.

The visual representation of the money problem along with the numerical division sentence gave meaning to the concept of division and further set the stage for the new learning. The Do Now also included two levels of difficulty—one dividing by $.50, the other more difficult task, dividing by $.75. This simple extension differentiated the problem and achieved the same instructional goal. Each day the Do Now offered similar differentiation. The teacher continued to offer the fraction tiles to those students who needed the concrete materials. By building in support, the learning of students who struggle with math is accelerated, and the need for constant reteaching is diminished. The fraction tiles serve as a concrete visual as well as a meaningful application of the concept of division. This is an especially effective technique for ELL students (Ovando, Collier, & Combs, 2003).

Each of the lessons over the three days focused on meaningful learning rather than rote memorization. The teacher on Day 1 could have stated, "You know how to multiply fractions. Today you will divide fractions. Step 1: Change all numbers into a proper fraction. Step 2: Invert the second fraction. Step 3: Proceed as if it were multiplication." The result of such instruction is some retention for students who respond to procedural instruction and who have good memories. For students who need concrete representation or who do not easily remember procedures, misconceptions result. Without solid understanding, there will be no positive transfer to use in future lessons when the teacher introduces solving problems related to division of fractions. Problem solving requires that students construct a mental representation, in this case the visual and concrete models. It is the student, not the teacher, who must work through and solve the problem (Mayer, 1992, 2002).

The homework assignment on the first day posed an open-ended question, "Do you see a pattern for dividing fractions using multiplication?" The teacher differentiated this assignment for special education, ELL, and SEL students by including a visual scaffolding tool to reinforce the concept of division through additional patterns. According to Ovando et al. (2003), when teachers consistently use scaffolding supports, the learning of ELL students accelerates in content area subjects. Additionally, the teacher followed a structured semantic model (Ovando et al., 2003) when introducing the new vocabulary word, *reciprocal*. She engaged the students in a series of problems to develop the word in context; students repeated the word and engaged in an oral dialog immediately after introducing the vocabulary word.

The group work on Day 3 involved a jigsaw model. Heterogeneous groups initially solved a problem together to become "experts" for that problem. Each group member then moved to a new group to share that expertise with peers. This cooperative learning strategy actively involves all students in the lesson and allows the teacher to check for understanding and offer assistance where needed.

The last homework assignment, Figure 2.3, focused on vocabulary. Too often in mathematics, this literacy component is ignored to the detriment of the students. Just as a student must know and understand the terms in biology, so must they know and understand the math terms to be able to read, comprehend, and solve problems. The optional musical problem offered a higher level application of solving a problem using the concepts of fractions and division.

Implications for Acceleration

By the end of Grade 5, the compacted curriculum includes all operations with fractions. These operations are taught in a meaningful manner to promote positive transfer and retention. The skills and concepts will be spiraled and reinforced throughout the year. When students move to Grade 6, teachers will not reintroduce fractions but rather apply them as needed to new topics. The sixth-grade teacher will spiral questions relating to the operations of fractions and the understanding of fractions from the beginning of the school year. The spiral activities can be part of a homework assignment or included in preparation for state assessment. A suggestion for homework assignments is to include five examples from the objective of the day, two from the previous day's objective, and two from previously taught objectives. Bimonthly assignments that include previously taught material in the format of state assessments have a two-fold benefit— consistent reinforcement and review of topics and better test scores. By combining compacted curriculum with lessons that teach for deep understanding, teachers in Grade 6 can teach all rational numbers including integer operations which are typically taught in Grade 7, and thus accelerate student learning.

Each district must examine its own curriculum to determine topics to compact. The overarching principle is that when a topic is introduced, develop the topic for full understanding. Don't teach a *part* of division of fractions. Don't teach only addition and subtraction of integers. Finish the topic. Allow the students to develop a full understanding in a developmentally sound manner.

ACCELERATING LEARNING BY DEVELOPING THE GIFTS AND TALENTS OF ALL STUDENTS

We began this chapter by describing the Accelerated Schools Movement and how Hank Levin (1998) courageously asserted that the education for "the best" was the best education for all. Renzulli's Schoolwide Enrichment Model (SEM) is an excellent source of ideas on how to accelerate learning through enrichment. The collected body of research on SEM suggests that the instructional pedagogy often reserved for a select few students labeled as gifted and talented can and should be employed throughout a school to extend enrichment-based opportunities to all students. When teachers employ such teaching practices, students achieve as well or better than when traditional or remedial strategies are utilized (Reis, n.d; Reis et al., 1998).

Elementary schools can have inclusive, rather than exclusive gifted programs based on the SEM model. Such is the case in the Rockville Centre, New York School District (Burris & Garrity, 2008, 2009). We believe that it is the responsibility of each educator to identify and nurture the gifts and talents of all students using SEM as a strategy in mainstream classes.

SEM includes both individual and group activities that are clustered into three categories or types. Type I general exploratory activities expose students to experiences such as visiting authors and artists. Type II group activities develop critical thinking, research, and communicative skills—skills that are critical for college and career success. Type III individual and small group experiences engage students in advanced study and research in an area that interests them. Teachers gently guide students based on their areas of interest and talents (Burris & Garrity, 2008, 2009).

Model Lesson: A Third Grade Literacy Extension - Type II

Analyze how two or more texts address similar themes or topics in order to build knowledge or to compare the approaches the authors take.

National Governors Association,
CCSS for ELA, Anchor Standards for Reading,
College and Career Readiness, p. 10

To build a foundation for college and career readiness, students must have ample opportunities to take part in a variety of rich, structured conversations—as part of a whole class, in small groups, and with a partner. Being productive members of these conversations requires that students contribute accurate, relevant information; respond to and develop what others have said; make comparisons and contrasts; and analyze and synthesize a multitude of ideas in various domains.

> National Governors Association,
> CCSS for ELA, Anchor Standards for Speaking and
> Listening, College and Career Readiness,
> Note on range and content, p. 22

Successful student employ reading skills and strategies to understand literature. They engage in an analytic process to enhance comprehension and create personal meaning when reading text.

> *Understanding University Success,* p. 22

Most schools use an anthology or basal reading program as the primary resource for reading instruction. This lesson is an example of how a reading lesson from the grade-level reader taught by the classroom teacher can be extended and enriched to develop critical reading skills, higher level thinking, and oral communication skills in students.

The lesson began with the classroom teacher and the students reading *The Keeping Quilt* (2001) by Patricia Polacco as part of the prescribed literacy program. The enrichment teacher extended the lessons for students by using the story to introduce and apply the reading strategy of making connections and to engage the students in a book talk discussion.

Prior to the lesson, the enrichment teacher gathered picture books on a range of reading and interest levels by the same author, Patricia Polacco. She then taught the class a mini lesson using a picture book by a different author. During the lesson, she modeled how to make connections before reading using the book title and cover illustrations. Her connections to the book were personal, which made students comfortable when it was their turn to share. Students then entered the conversation by adding their own life connections.

The teacher explained how making connections before, during, and after reading helps them to better understand the story. She then read aloud the picture book to the class. As she made a connection, she jotted the information on a sticky note and placed it in the text. When she finished the read aloud, the students wrote at least one connection that they made with the story, shared this with a partner, and explained how the connection helped them better understand a part of the story (Robb,

(Continued)

(Continued)

2006). The enrichment teacher and the classroom teacher paired each student with a Polacco book based on reading ability and interest. The teachers, using Figure 2.4, modeled a book talk during which they named types of connections; compared illustrations, characters, and the theme with *The Keeping Quilt*; and offered a book review of their selected book.

During the next three days, students read their selected book during independent reading time. They made sticky notes to mark connections and recorded notes in their reading journals. Students used Figure 2.5 if needed. The ELL and special education teachers assisted their students using Figures 2.4 and 2.5. On the fourth day, each student completed a Book Talk form as a tool to guide his or her participation in the book talk the following day. In groups of four, students presented their Polacco book, identified connections, compared their book to *The Keeping Quilt*, and offered an overall book review. Group members asked questions and offered additional connections and comparisons.

The picture books remained in the classroom for an additional week to allow students to read other books by the author. As a further extension, some students wrote and illustrated a picture book related to a special tradition in their own family.

Figure 2.4 Personal Connections for Book Talk

Book Talk: Patricia Polacco

The Keeping Quilt and _____

I made "text to self" connections with my Patricia Polacco book. It reminded me of:
_____

I made "text to text" connections with my Patricia Polacco book. It reminded me of :
_____

Similarities

Differences

Illustrations

Characters

Lesson/Theme

I think other people should /should not read this book because:

_____

_____

_____

_____

Figure 2.5 Book Talk Guideline

Book Talk Process

- Each member of your group chooses one book by Patricia Polacco and reads it.
- While you read your book, take notes in your journal using the suggestions below.
- Use sticky notes to mark parts of the story to support your notes.

While reading your book by Patricia Polacco

- Try to make connections to your own life—a "text to self" connection. Does something in your book remind you of something in your life, your family? Have you had a similar experience?
- Try to make connections to another book—a "text to text" connection. Does this book remind you of another book? How?
- Think about how your book is the **same** and how it is **different** from *The Keeping Quilt.*

    1. Look at the illustrations. Does the author use the same style as in *The Keeping Quilt*?

    2. What about the characters? Are they members of her family? If not, describe them.

(Continued)

(Continued)

3. Does Patricia Polacco try to teach you a lesson or give you an important message as she does in *The Keeping Quilt*? Remember, in *The Keeping Quilt* she really wanted us to know about the importance of **traditions.**

4. What other things did you notice?

• Do you think others should read this book? Why or why not?

Tips for Working in Your Group

• Take turns speaking.
• Prepare your notes in your journal.
• Use your notes during your discussion.
• Support your ideas with details from the story.

Reflection on the Lesson

The grade-level literacy program provides the standard level of instruction for teachers. This series of lessons offers a means of providing enriched and interesting instruction in specific reading strategies to all students by using alternative reading material above and below grade level. Instead of segregating students by reading levels for remediation or enrichment, all students participated in a valuable class experience sharing in rich book talk discussions while meeting the lesson goals with or without scaffolding materials. We know that it is critical for our English language learners to participate in rich literacy environments rather than to always be isolated in ELL classrooms or to be mainstreamed into low-track classes (Freeman & Freeman, 2009). The same is true for our SEL learners and our special education students who need enriched learning environments to catch up (Zweirs, 2008).

When readers make connections that are related to them, to another text, or to an event, they are more likely to understand the author's purpose, a character's actions, and the overall story (Harvey & Goudvis, 2000). Like our first example in this chapter, using what is of interest to students is a powerful motivator. In this lesson, the teachers are consciously linking students' experiences to new learning and explicitly teaching students the strategy by name to foster and reinforce positive transfer.

During the mini lessons, the teacher involves students in the process. Support for struggling students is provided by a written guide sheet to prepare them for working independently. Students' learning is facilitated when a teacher models a strategy and talks about it using a shared language. The ELL and special education teachers reinforce this model working with their students on the guide sheet. Learning is enhanced when students have the opportunity to hear classmates approach a task (Pintrich, 2002).

Prior to this experience, students should use the compare and contrast strategy in literacy work. This provides a comfort level for the book talk. In addition, as students become more adept at discussing similarities and differences in literacy, they begin to use these skills across the curriculum in all content area subjects. Again, this builds on prior knowledge to accelerate learning.

CLOSING THOUGHTS ON ACCELERATION

The examples provided in this chapter are intended to help the reader understand how the principles of accelerated learning can be integrated into lessons and curriculum. The presented strategies range from the conscious use of transfer to curriculum compacting and enrichment. We ask that you remember what we said in the beginning of this chapter: *Accelerated instruction is not about racing through the curriculum. Rather, it is about the maximal use of instructional time for each individual student in order to accelerate his or her learning.* The purpose is to bring all children to college and career readiness, rather than leave some children further and further behind. If we are to have prepared students, we must deliberately infuse the experiences that they need in a methodical and deliberate way K–12. It cannot be left to chance, nor can it be left to the final years of high school.

Here are some questions to think about as you develop your lessons with the intent of accelerating your students' learning.

Reflective Questions for Accelerated Teaching

- Did I account for the multiple talents and challenges that my students possess in the development of my lesson?
- How did CCSS and KSUS inform my planning?
- Is the material of high interest to students?
- How can I build on prior knowledge and use of transfer to accelerate learning?
- Do I know what errors or misunderstandings some or all students will likely experience? If so, what is my plan for addressing these errors?

- How will I monitor student learning? What feedback do I want my coteacher or assistant to give me?
- How can I use assessment to help compact lessons and units?
- What are alternative explanations, examples, and models that can be used in this lesson or in support classes to further understanding? What materials should I share with the special education and ELL teachers so that they can support our students?
- How can I make enriched lessons following the SEM model accessible for all of the students in my class?
- What scaffolding have I provided to allow all students to experience an enriched learning experience?
- How do I ensure that students develop a deep understanding?
- How can I fully develop topics in order to reduce the need for reteaching?

If you are unsure of how to answer some of the questions above, do not worry! In subsequent chapters we will provide additional strategies to promote the college and career ready skills students need when they leave us. One of the best tools that we know to provide a lift in challenge to any lesson is the skilful use of Bloom's Taxonomy of the Cognitive Domain. How teachers can effectively use the taxonomy to develop students' critical thinking skills will be the theme of the next chapter.

3 Critical Thinking Skills—The *C* in ACES

CRITICAL THINKING AND POSTSECONDARY EXPECTATIONS

When you ask most adults who their favorite teacher was, someone always comes to mind. And when you ask them why they liked that teacher so much, the answer usually sounds something like this, "He made me believe that I was smart!" or "She really made me think!" If you probe a little deeper, you may hear how that teacher made learning enjoyable or accessible, but it is unlikely that you will hear an adult respond, "I liked him because he was easy and I did not have to think very much."

The engagement of the mind makes learning enjoyable and class time flies. When we are not challenged and we are bored, learning becomes painful and time drags on at an unbearable pace. Engaging students in critical thinking, also known as higher level thinking, is not only motivational, it is the best way that we can prepare our students for postsecondary education and for the 21st century workplace.

In the introduction to *Understanding University Success*, Conley (2003) discusses how important it is that schools develop the "habits of mind" that students need in college—habits that college professors deem to be even more important than knowledge of content (p. 9). Not surprisingly, the abilities to think critically about content and to analyze, synthesize, draw inferences, and evaluate sources are identified as important skills across the curricula. In addition, critical thinking and decision making were two of the most important skills needed for the 21st century workplace as well (Achieve and the Education Trust, 2008).

The Common Core (National Governors Association, 2010) emphasizes the importance of critical thinking skills. The reading standards, for example, require students to interpret, analyze, and evaluate what they read. Higher level thinking skills weave through all of the English language arts standards. In fact, if there is one major difference between the Common Core and present state standards, it is the emphasis that the Core places on high level thinking, especially analysis (Porter, McMaken, Hwang, & Yang, 2011).

At this point, the skeptical reader is probably questioning both the validity and feasibility of the advice given by those who created Knowledge and Skills for University Success (KSUS) (Conley, 2003) and those who developed the Common Core State Standards (CCSS). Is this advice intended only for high achieving students? How can students think critically absent content? And, if students struggle with content, how can we expect them to engage in higher level thinking skills?

First, if the skill of being able to think critically were only relevant to high-achieving students in high-track classes, we would not include it in this book. All classrooms K–12, especially heterogeneous classes, are the perfect setting to expand our students' ability to think. What we presently do in most schools, which is to develop the critical thinking skills of the few, must change if all students are prepared for postsecondary success (Burris & Garrity, 2009).

Second, we agree that students cannot think critically without content knowledge. How we teach content, however, can be altered to develop skill along with knowledge. This is exactly what Conley (2003) in *Understanding University Success* advocates:

> Understanding and mastery of the content knowledge… is achieved through the exercise of broader cognitive skills. It is not enough simply to know something; the learner must possess the ability to do something with that knowledge, whether it is to solve a problem, reach a conclusion or present a point of view. (p. 9)

Finally, for students who struggle, it is possible to engage in complex, higher level thinking. Complexity is not synonymous with difficulty. Learning can be difficult without being complex, and the reverse is also true—learning can be very complex but not difficult.

We will explain. Here are two hypothetical homework assignments. We often ask teachers, given a choice, which would you choose? The first is: *Memorize the 206 bones of the human body.* The second assignment is: *Analyze the complexity level of a lesson that you taught yesterday, using Bloom's Taxonomy as a guide.*

As you might imagine, nearly everyone we ask chooses the second assignment. The first assignment does not engage the learner in higher order thinking. The learner engages in remembering (low complexity), but the assignment is very difficult because it requires that the learner memorize many items in a short period of time. The second assignment requires higher level thinking (analysis), but given knowledge of Bloom's Taxonomy, which most teachers have, as well as familiar content of their own lessons, it is not very difficult. If we were to change the first assignment to *memorize the fourteen bones in the human face,* the level of difficulty would decrease and the low level of complexity would remain the same. Likewise, if the second assignment were to analyze a colleague's teaching unit using Bloom, the difficulty of that assignment would increase, but the level of complexity would remain the same.

By carefully calibrating the level of difficulty, higher levels of complexity become more or less accessible to students. Given the proper supports and the right level of difficulty, all students, including those who struggle, can develop their critical thinking skills. According to Zweirs (2008), the vocabulary of critical thinking and the phrases needed to describe abstraction can be taught to English language learners (ELLs) and Standard English learners (SELs) to help them better describe their thinking. With the right supports and strategies, critical thinking can become an integral part of K–12 lessons.

The integration of thinking skills, however, is not something to be done on the fly. Thoughtful planning, using Bloom's Taxonomy of the Cognitive Domain, can help us design lessons that develop the higher level thinking skills of our students even as we teach them the content they need to know. In addition, it can serve as an important check to ensure that activities, objectives, and assessments are aligned (Raths, 2002). Before we discuss how to infuse critical thinking skills in lessons, it is important that we develop a shared vocabulary and structure for lesson planning. As in the implementation of all instructional changes, lesson planning is key!

BASICS OF LESSON PLANNING

Good teaching begins with thoughtful planning. The renowned educational researcher Madeline Hunter once told one of us that it takes four times as long to plan a good lesson as it does to teach it (Hunter, 1982). Although it is impossible to spend so much time on every lesson, if you want to produce a truly outstanding lesson, Dr. Hunter's estimate is probably not far off the mark. Indeed, in the Japanese practice of lesson study, 10–15 hours are devoted to the creation, critiquing, and revision of the lesson (Fernandez, 2002).

However, we know that most American teachers do not put much time into lesson creation—either they do not formally plan lessons, or their planning is inadequate (Stigler & Hiebert, 1999). As teachers become more experienced, often simple notes to self based on last year's lesson substitute for planning. Even as teaching in isolation characterizes our schools, so does planning in isolation. Communication about planning often consists of "What are you doing today?" as teachers hurry to class or chat in the teacher's lounge. Time is the enemy, and so lessons, with their accompanying worksheets, are recycled.

The basic model of the lesson plan, based on Hunter's six-step model, (found in Figure 3.1) provides a good foundation for instructional planning. Like a good story, a lesson needs an intriguing beginning, a logical unfolding, and a conclusion that brings students to understanding. The objective serves as the plot that brings both purpose and coherence to the lesson. Often the inclination is to search for interesting activities and then build the lesson around them, thus confusing activities with learning goals (Anderson & Krathwohl, 2001). Objectives must come first, and as the reader will see as this chapter develops, it is within that objective that the level of complexity of the lesson is set.

Figure 3.1 Foundational Elements of a Lesson Plan Based on the Madeline Hunter Model

- Good lessons begin with a thoughtful lesson **objective** which clearly describes what students will learn and be able to do in order to demonstrate that learning. All other parts of the lesson plan should flow from that objective. It is often expressed as a learning **aim,** which is a question or statement shared with the class at the start of the lesson. Teachers return to the **aim** at the end of the lesson in order to gauge student understanding.
- The **anticipatory set** is an activity or question that is designed to capture student attention and to direct their attention to the lesson objective.
- **Input** is the term used to describe that part of the lesson during which students are introduced to new learning. Strategies may include an investigation, lecture, Socratic questioning, readings, film, etc. Modeling, which is often part of input, occurs when the teacher presents a model to enhance student learning or as the first opportunity for student practice. It can be a step by step solution to a math problem for example, or a diagram, or a demonstration. The model shows students what the teacher expects in subsequent practice.
- **In guided practice,** under the direction of the teacher, students practice to ensure retention of the learning and to show mastery.
- **Closure** occurs in the mind of the learner. The teacher prompts the students to internalize the concepts taught in a coherent and organized way. It should reinforce the learning, and clear up misconceptions.
- **Independent practice** is practice without the guidance of the teacher. Generally it is homework.

The Hunter model, which was developed in the 1970s and 1980s, brought structure and coherence to our understanding of teaching and learning. Hunter's genius was her ability to observe excellent teachers, note what they did, and then describe effective teaching practices based on learning theory. From those descriptions, a common vocabulary to describe instruction was born. We will use that basic vocabulary, given in Figure 3.1, in our descriptions of lessons as we proceed.

As helpful as the Hunter model still is, much has changed since it was developed. Differentiated instruction was not part of educational theory or practice, and special education students were isolated in self-contained classes. Clearly, we need to supplement and enrich the basic model if we are to bring diverse learners to high achievement. One strategy for doing so is to examine each part of the lesson through the prism of Bloom's Taxonomy.

Let's begin, then with a basic lesson that follows the Hunter lesson design model. We will then discuss Bloom's Taxonomy, analyze the lesson using the taxonomy, and then infuse critical thinking into the lesson.

Lesson on Feudalism (1)

Below is a social studies lesson on the topic of feudalism designed for ninth-grade students. We will use this lesson as a model to show how a traditional lesson can be progressively transformed into a lesson that provides challenging yet accessible learning to all students.

The **objective** of this introductory lesson is to provide students with an understanding of the system of feudalism as it existed in Western Europe. At the beginning of the lesson, students are introduced to an **aim**: *Evaluate whether the system of feudalism brought progress to Western Europe.*

The teacher engages in a quick skit in which he pretends to be a serf that has just been sold with the land on which he farms. The skit is dramatic and humorous and serves as the **anticipatory set** for the lesson.

The teacher provides **input** by showing a series of PowerPoint slides to the class. Each student has a graphic organizer handout on which to record notes. Slides include definitions of vocabulary terms, descriptions of feudal classes, and basic information about how feudalism worked. Some slides include illustrations. The teacher then presents a PowerPoint slide showing a model of feudalism—a pyramid that has multiple compartments. Each class title of the feudal era is listed in a different compartment, with the king at the apex and the peasants and serfs in the base. During the presentation of each slide, the teacher asks who, what, and yes or no questions to check for understanding.

For **guided practice**, the teacher gives each student a role that reflects a feudal class (king, peasant, and knight, for example). They are told to find a classmate either above or below them on the pyramid and come to an agreement on what they will give and receive in their feudal relationship. If they cannot come to agreement, they move on to another student until they do. For example, the king comes to an agreement with a noble regarding how much land he will give in exchange for protection. The purpose of this activity is to understand how each class was dependent on the other for wealth, protection, crops, and so forth.

As the class comes to a close, the teacher brings the class's attention back to the **aim** that serves as **closure.** Students share their opinion on whether or not feudalism brought progress to Western Europe as a *yes* or *no* response. For homework, the teacher asks the class to write a paragraph to support their opinion. The class concludes.

Reflection on the lesson

The above lesson contains all of the foundational elements of a good lesson. It includes visual presentations, writing, and cooperative work. All of the parts of the Hunter model are present. The activities in the lesson are related to the objective, which has a sound curricular foundation. Despite these strengths, the lesson does not engage the learners in speculative thinking, analytical activities, and open-ended questions that promote critical thinking. Although the closure question and homework assignment are intended to engage students in critical thinking, the activities of the lesson do not promote higher level thought. It is doubtful that all students will be able to respond to the aim in a truly evaluative way. This is because the lesson does not provide the instructional support needed to do so. Students are never asked to grapple with the big questions. What do we mean by progress? How can we evaluate whether societal progress has occurred? As the lesson stands, it will be difficult for students to make an evaluative judgment.

Will some high achieving students be able to respond to the aim and do the homework in a way that reflects deep understanding and critical thinking? Perhaps. Some talented students might be able to provide a meaningful response because of outside reading, interest, or exposure to evaluative questions. The aim of this chapter, however, is to provide insight into how to develop the critical thinking skills of *all* students.

It is important for students to learn the historical facts and concepts embedded in the lesson, and in that regard, the lesson is effective. Classrooms that are designed to make all students college and career ready, however, use the acquisition of knowledge not as an end but also as a means to develop the higher level thinking skills that are needed for postsecondary success. This does not make learning more difficult, but it does make it more complex. How to identify and increase the complexity of our lessons and create experiences that will engage the minds of our students in higher level thinking is the topic of the following section.

BLOOM'S TAXONOMY AND HIGHER LEVEL THINKING

One of the best tools we have for developing critical thinking skills is Bloom's Taxonomy of the Cognitive Domain, a system that classifies learning objectives and activities by the kind of thinking that they require. The original taxonomy was published in 1956 in a volume that was edited by educational psychologist Benjamin Bloom. Bloom envisioned his taxonomy not only as a tool for the measurement of learning, but as the beginning of a common language to be used by educators so that they could readily communicate about learning goals, curricula, standards, and assessments (Krathwohl, 2002).

The taxonomy, as originally designed by Bloom and his colleagues, consisted of six categories arranged in a hierarchy of increasing complexity. The first category, deemed to be the least complex in terms of cognitive processing, was knowledge. Knowledge was followed in the taxonomy by comprehension, application, analysis, synthesis, and evaluation—with evaluation considered to be the most complex form of thinking. According to Bloom, each step up the hierarchy assumed that the prior level had been mastered (Bloom, 1956). For example, if students *comprehend* that water will result when they melt an ice cube, it is because they *know* that ice is frozen water.

After considerable study by an assembly of psychologists, researchers, and other educational experts, a revision to the taxonomy was published in 2001. In the revised taxonomy, knowledge is no longer the first level. Rather, this taxonomy is two dimensional, distinguishing different types of knowledge—factual knowledge, conceptual knowledge, procedural knowledge, and metacognitive knowledge. The four kinds of knowledge and a description of each can be found in Figure 3.2 (Anderson & Krathwohl, 2001; Krathwhol, 2002).

Like the original taxonomy, it also identifies the cognitive processes and orders them by level of complexity (see Figure 3.3). In the revised version, evaluation and synthesis exchange places, and the nouns that describe each level are replaced by verbs. *Knowledge* became *remember*, *comprehension* became *understand*, *application* became *apply*, *analysis* became *analyze*, *evaluation* became *evaluate* and *synthesis* became *create* (Anderson & Krathwohl, 2001; Krathwohl, 2002).

Figure 3.2 The Four Kinds of Knowledge Identified by the Revised Taxonomy

Knowledge type	Description
Factual knowledge	Elements and facts to be known by students such as terminology, definitions, dates, etc.
Conceptual knowledge	Knowledge of the relationships that connect elemental facts into big ideas. Conceptual knowledge includes knowledge of principles, categories, theories, models, and other schema.
Procedural knowledge	Knowledge of how to do something such as solving a problem, conducting an experiment, or playing a sport. Includes knowledge of techniques, skills, procedures, methods, etc.
Metacognitive knowledge	Knowledge of thinking, including one's own cognitive processes. Includes knowledge of strategies as well as knowledge of self.

Figure 3.3 The Revised Taxonomy of the Cognitive Domain

	Factual Knowledge	Conceptual Knowledge	Procedural Knowledge	Metacognitive Knowledge
create				
evaluate				
analyze				
apply				
understand				
remember				

With the revision of the taxonomy, learning objectives—whether they are lesson or unit objectives—can be more finely defined by both complexity of thinking and by knowledge type. For example, *students will write a persuasive essay on why freedom of speech is critical to a democracy* would require students to engage in the highest cognitive process, create (*write a persuasive essay*), and require them to have both factual as well as conceptual knowledge components (*why freedom of speech is critical to a democracy*). Not only would they need to have a deep understanding of concepts such as freedom of speech and democracy, they would need factual knowledge to make a sound, persuasive argument.

On the other hand, an objective such as *students will write a five paragraph essay* is a very different task. The cognitive process requires understanding (*the function of each of the five paragraphs*), but this objective does not require the critical thinking skills needed to achieve the previous objective. In this objective, the teacher is focusing on the development of a skill, which requires procedural knowledge (*how to write a five paragraph essay*).

Here is an additional example intended to provide clarification. Let's suppose that a third-grade class investigates butterflies as part of a cross-disciplinary unit that combined art, science, and literacy. At the end of the unit, the students imagine that they were a butterfly and write and illustrate a storybook of their life. The cognitive activity associated with this assignment would involve higher level thinking skills, and the objective for that lesson could be classified as *conceptual knowledge* or *create* on the revised taxonomy. If the teacher were to provide instruction in letter writing, and then asked the class to write a letter to a friend about butterflies, that would be classified as *procedural knowledge* or *apply*. Both are writing tasks and may have objectives that include the word *write* as the verb, but both are at very different levels of the taxonomy.

Although initially the two dimensional taxonomy can be challenging to use, it is a great tool to help us analyze the thinking skills that students will use during our lessons. By way of illustration, let's use what we have learned about the revised taxonomy to analyze the lesson on feudalism which was introduced earlier in the chapter. We will use the taxonomy to classify the level of complexity of the thinking that students will engage in during each part of the lesson, as well the type of knowledge they are gaining. Results of the analysis are recorded in Figure 3.4. To help distinguish between the two dimensions of the revised taxonomy, we put the cognitive process in bold type and the knowledge type in italics.

REEXAMINING THE FIRST LESSON ON FEUDALISM

The objective of a lesson frames the intended learning outcome. In this case, the lesson objective was the following:

> *Students will understand the system of feudalism as it existed in Western Europe during the Medieval Ages.*

Feudalism and the relationships among the groups that existed under it can be described as *conceptual* knowledge. The objective, therefore, can be classified as **understand** *conceptual* knowledge. The anticipatory set (A.S.) is a short skit that illustrates how serfs were bound to the land of the lord of the manor and were transferred with the land if that land were sold or confiscated. The purpose was to help students understand a societal position that they have not encountered before, that of the serf. Therefore, it can be classified as **understand** *conceptual* knowledge.

Teacher input is provided by informational slides from which students copy notes. The teacher also presents a simple model of feudal class hierarchy and asks who, why, what, yes, or no questions to check for understanding. The recording of notes is intended to facilitate **remembering** *factual* knowledge, and the model and questions are to check for **understanding** of *conceptual* knowledge.

Guided practice (students writing contracts) gives students opportunity to **apply** what they have learned. Because students apply what they learn, the cognitive processes used during this part of the lesson are best described as **applying** *conceptual* knowledge.

The lesson's closure activity asks students to respond to the lessons aim:

> Evaluate whether the system of feudalism brought progress to Western Europe.

Students would engage in **evaluative** thinking—they would judge whether or not feudalism brought progress to Western Europe (*conceptual* knowledge). Given the previous learning activities, however, is evaluative thinking supported by the lesson?

Figure 3.4 maps out where in the taxonomy each of the parts of the lesson falls. Notice the jump from the guided practice activity to the closure. In this lesson, students never engage in an analysis of feudalism. They are not given criteria by which to make a judgment and so students will not be able to give more than an opinion. Although the closure activity has the potential to spark higher level thinking at the level of evaluation, it is not organically connected to the lesson and therefore will not bring students to the intended level of thinking. Too much was skipped along the way!

The lesson did not include an analysis of the social structure of feudalism, a comparison with the social structure of Western Europe that preceded feudalism, nor an operational definition of progress. Often, well-meaning teachers will include higher level questions and activities, but not provide the experiences or scaffolding for students to answer them. The danger of such a practice is that students can begin to believe that just giving their opinion is enough. Later, when they are asked to write evaluative essays in college, they are dumbfounded when their papers are not well received. Mapping out objectives and activities on Bloom can help teachers see gaps in their lessons as well as discover opportunities to make their lessons more complex.

PLANNING LESSONS TO DEVELOP CRITICAL THINKING

Bloom's Taxonomy of the Cognitive Domain is a powerful tool in helping us design lessons that develop the thinking skills of our students. The

Figure 3.4 Taxonomy of the Cognitive Domain and the Original Lesson

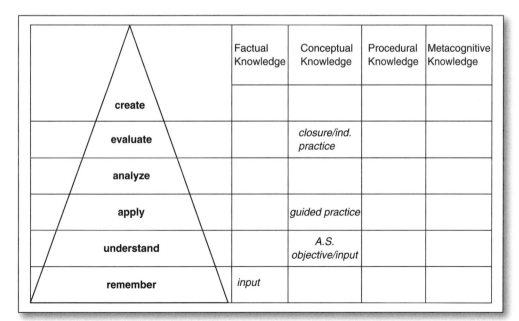

	Factual Knowledge	Conceptual Knowledge	Procedural Knowledge	Metacognitive Knowledge
create				
evaluate		closure/ind. practice		
analyze				
apply		guided practice		
understand		A.S. objective/input		
remember	input			

taxonomy can be used not only to help create objectives that support high student achievement, but as a tool to check for consistency among objectives, activities, pedagogy, and assessment (Anderson & Krathwohl, 2001). Here are questions to ask to guide the development of objectives and experiences that are on a higher cognitive level.

- Does the activity require some mastery of the levels below for students to have success at the higher level? Bloom envisioned each level of the taxonomy to be cumulative, encompassing the levels beneath it (Krathwohl, 2002).
- What will occur in the minds of the learners? Will they make new connections with old learning for example, or will they simply practice what you present?
- How much variation will there be in outcomes that result from the activity? The more similar student output, the less complex the activity.
- How will you assess the final product? If you find yourself struggling to create a complex rubric for assessment, then the task is probably of a higher level.

Before we return to our original lesson and infuse it with critical thinking, it is important to reflect on what we know about how students learn. Learning is a dynamic, active process that must engage the minds of the learners. In addition, everything our students learn is affected by what they have learned before, that is, consciously and unconsciously, learners test all new knowledge against the beliefs and constructs that they have already developed. This is the process of transfer, which was discussed in Chapter 1. As we revise the lesson, we will seek to include more opportunity for active learning even as we increase the opportunity for critical thinking.

REVISED LESSON ON FEUDALISM (2)

Successful students know significant periods and events in world history and social, religious and political movements, as well as major historical figures who influenced such movements. They understand the social, economic and political climate of significant periods in history and how a particular climate shaped those who live at the time.

Understanding University Success, p. 61

Initiate and participate effectively in a range of collaborative discussions (one-on-one, in groups, and teacher-led) with diverse
partners on grades 9–10 topics, texts, and issues, building on others' ideas and expressing their own clearly and persuasively.…
Respond thoughtfully to diverse perspectives, summarize points
of agreement and disagreement, and, when warranted, qualify or
justify their own views and understanding and make new connections in light of the evidence and reasoning presented.

National Governors Association, CCSS for English Language
Arts: Comprehension and Collaboration (Grades 9–10), p. 50

As mentioned earlier in this chapter, every lesson plan should start
with a learning goal or objective that guides the development of all learning experiences. We often tell new teachers to imagine that each student
enters their class with a large basket in hand. It is the teacher's job to fill
that basket with meaningful learning. In addition, students should be able
to explain what they are holding as they walk out the classroom door, as
well as why having the filled basket matters.

If we review the original lesson, we can glean what the teacher hoped
would be in each learner's basket. From the original objective, we know
that the teacher wanted students to understand how feudalism functioned.
The aim suggests that he also wanted students to look at the feudal system
with a critical eye—he hoped to engage students in critical thinking about
the topic, making a judgment as to whether feudalism was a more progres-
sive system than the system which preceded it. Although it may be too
ambitious to expect ninth graders to evaluate a political system, it is not
unreasonable to expect them to analyze some aspects of the system, provided they are given materials and instructional support at the correct
level of difficulty.

In the original lesson, the teacher did provide information that had the
potential of helping students evaluate feudalism in meaningful ways. He
included a guided practice activity to help students understand that inter-
dependent exchanges among the groups gave structure to the feudal system. As in all social systems, however, each group did not equally benefit.
The following is a revised, less ambitious **objective** for the lesson:

Students will be able to determine the extent to which different
groups benefitted from feudalism in Western Europe.

This objective can now be turned into a relevant aim question to help
students and their teacher assess learning:

During feudalism, which social class benefited the most and which class benefitted the least? Justify your answer.

Now that the objective is determined, the teacher must create the experiences and activities needed for students to achieve it. The original lesson assumed that students had no prior knowledge of feudalism. Should we assume that students know nothing about the topic? Is there a way that we can engage students in the retrieval of information early in the lesson?

Feudalism is introduced in the elementary social studies curriculum, and it is reasonable to assume that students are familiar with at least some of the terms associated with the era such as knights, castles, and serfs. The revised lesson, then, begins with this **anticipatory set** activity that is designed to spark transfer of prior knowledge:

Write a list of four words or ideas that come to mind when you hear the word feudalism.

This activity serves several important functions. First, because all students are required to participate, the level of active processing is high. Second, it allows the teacher to clear up any misconceptions that students might have (negative transfer) as well as identify areas that might need to be emphasized. The teacher can either make an adjustment in the lesson or make a mental note for follow-up the next day. Third, the teacher can also identify what prior knowledge and understandings that he can build on and use during the lesson. Finally, this act of recall is in itself a learning event and increases the odds that information will be retrieved at a later time. Asking students to dig deep and remember is a powerful learning tool (National Research Council, 1991; Rohrer & Pashler, 2010).

In the original lesson, **input** was provided by displaying slides, and it was required that students record notes. The revised lessons will use a more active, student-centered approach. Students will be assigned one of three handouts which they will closely read and to which they will respond. They will have about fifteen minutes to complete this task. Each handout is designed to provide important information to achieve the lesson objective. This activity is designed to moderate the level of difficulty so that all students can have access to the learning objective. Below is a description of each.

Handout 1: This handout is a more sophisticated version of the simple model used in the original lesson. Rather than a simple triangle with sections, this diagram provides extensive information about feudal structure. It is designed for students who do better with organizational charts than with extended prose. Such groups might include our ESL or SEL students who struggle with extended reading, or students who have difficulty organizing information obtained from text. An example of such a handout is given in Figure 3.5. Questions to answer with the handout would require students to determine which group determines the protection given to the kingdom, which group controls the flow of food, who distributes land, and so on.

Handout 2: This would be a one-page description of the feudal system and how it functioned during the Middle Ages in Western Europe. It would explain the relationships among the groups—especially the social and economic plight of the serfs. Definitions of the academic vocabulary terms *manorialism, serf, vassal, homage, fealty,* and *fief* will be embedded in the reading. Students who have this handout are required to extract those definitions and answer questions at their level of comprehension regarding the roles of each of the classes. This handout is designed for students who are effective readers and who have the skill to extract information from text.

Handout 3: This is a one and a half page description of the conditions that gave rise to feudalism. Students will have to closely read the text and infer information regarding the relative weakness of the king, the consequences of holding large land tracts during an era of poor transportation, the importance of protection following the fall of the Roman Empire, and the rise of the nobility. The questions asked will require them to draw conclusions regarding the above. They will sum up their conclusions. This handout is designed for students with excellent reading skills, especially the skills of inference and interpretation.

Guided practice: After students complete one of the above assignments, they will be assigned to cooperative groups composed of four students. Each group will have one student with Handout 1, one with Handout 3, and two with Handout 2. If the number of students present in the class is not divisible by four, one or more groups will have only one member with Handout 2. Students will have twelve minutes to share their responses with each other and to decide which group benefitted from feudalism the most, and which the least. Justification of the decision is based on relevant information in the handouts. As the students are working, the teacher passes out the additional handouts so that each student leaves class with all three.

Lesson closure: The teacher chooses one student from each of three groups to answer the aim question and justify the answer. In any remaining time, he leads the class in a fuller discussion and clears up any student misunderstandings.

Figure 3.5 Handout A

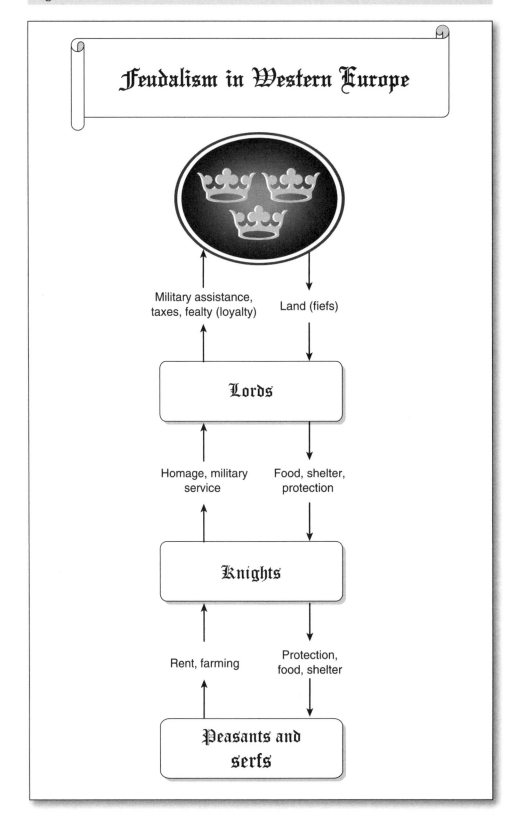

Independent practice: Homework consists of five questions for students to answer. To complete the assignment, students must reference all three handouts, their group notes, and notes on other political systems that they studied.

Analysis of the Revised Lesson Using the Taxonomy

Figure 3.6 lists some of the verbs associated with each level of the taxonomy, in order to help us determine the level of complexity.

The verb *determine*, which is in the revised objective, is associated with the revised Taxonomy's level entitled *analyze*, the first level of higher level cognitive processing (Mayer, 2002). Knowledge of how to classify or categorize is *conceptual knowledge* (Anderson & Krathwohl, 2001); therefore, this objective could be described as asking students to **analyze** *conceptual knowledge*. The aim question, which serves as closure, asks students to make a judgment and to justify their answer. Therefore, it can be classified as **evaluate** *conceptual knowledge*. Notice, however, that because it is more limited in scope (evaluating the benefits received by each class, rather than evaluating feudalism in the context of history), it is not as difficult as the aim of the first lesson, and is therefore achievable. Remember what we said earlier in this chapter—difficulty and complexity are not synonymous.

The anticipatory set (A.S.) is an activity of recall. It asks students to **remember** *factual knowledge*. Now let's take a look at the learning input. All three handouts are designed for understanding—of both factual and conceptual knowledge. What differs is the level of difficulty. The chart is the least difficult because the information is presented in a straightforward manner with visual as well as text cues. The third is the most difficult, because students must infer knowledge from the text. Unlike the first two, the extraction of knowledge is not straightforward. This is a good example of how teachers can differentiate

Figure 3.6 Verbs Associated With the Levels of the Taxonomy

Remember	Apply	Evaluate
Recall, identify, show	Solve, implement, practice, use	Judge, justify, critique, test, debate
Understand		
Explain, paraphrase, give an example of, summarize, classify, infer, compare, contrast	**Analyze** Take apart, differentiate, attribute, organize, determine	**Create** Produce, hypothesize, generate, plan

the level of difficulty, while keeping the same level of complexity for all. We can classify the activities as **understand** *factual and conceptual knowledge.*

The cooperative learning, guided practice (GP) requires students to analyze the knowledge that they have acquired and determine the degree to which each group benefitted from feudalism. Although the analysis of both factual and conceptual knowledge will take place, the resulting knowledge will be conceptual; therefore, this activity asks students to **analyze** *conceptual knowledge.* Finally, the closure activity, which asks students to answer the aim, requires students to **evaluate** the conclusions of their analysis. Because students analyzed the benefits of feudalism in a well-designed, cooperative activity, all students should now be ready to engage in the higher level, evaluative thinking that will result in high quality responses. The homework (independent practice) asks students to compare what they have learned about feudalism to other systems that they previously studied. Students will **apply** *both factual and conceptual knowledge* to complete the assignment.

The reader is encouraged to compare Figure 3.4 with Figure 3.7. Notice how the goals and activities of the second lesson gradually engage students in critical thinking. Cognitive complexity is gradually built during

Figure 3.7 Taxonomy of the Cognitive Domain and the Revised Lesson

	Factual Knowledge	Conceptual Knowledge	Procedural Knowledge	Metacognitive Knowledge
create				
evaluate		*Aim/Closure*		
analyze		*Obj.,Guided practice*		
apply	*Independent practice*	*Independent practice*		
understand	*Input*	*Input*		
remember	*Anticipatory set*			

the lesson. Further, because the level of difficulty is varied in the second lesson, more students can fully participate in it in a meaningful way. Higher achievers are challenged and students with reading difficulties can analyze the chart and provide meaningful contributions to the group work. The objective, which requires critical thinking, becomes achievable for all.

The second lesson also provides the instruction needed for students to answer the evaluative closure question of the first lesson. Let's suppose that in a subsequent lesson, the teacher asks the class to also analyze the social structure that existed prior to feudalism. This would serve as review, as well as an opportunity for students to practice the skills of analysis that they just learned. Transfer of knowledge from the feudalism lesson would accelerate student learning. The class, under the guidance of the teacher, could develop criteria by which to evaluate social progress in a society. Students would then have the tools that they needed to judge whether feudalism represented social progress in Western Europe during the Middle Ages.

DETERMINING THE LEVEL OF COMPLEXITY

Correctly classifying cognitive processes is not an exact science. Verb choice can also make classification difficult. Figure 3.6 gives a sample of verbs that are often associated with each level of cognitive complexity. If the word *evaluate* in the objective had been changed to *create*, one might misclassify the same activity on the highest level of the taxonomy. It is important, therefore, they we not fall into the trap of classifying objectives, activities, and assessments by verbs alone.

Here is an additional example for clarification. All four of the following activities use the verb *create:*

> Create a timeline for the completion of all of the steps you will need to accomplish to successfully complete your project.

> Create a timeline of the important events listed in Chapter 6 of your history textbook.

> Create a timeline for the significant life events of the protagonist of the short story that you are writing.

> Create a timeline of what you believe are the ten most significant events in American history based on their impact on the national economy. Justify their inclusion.

Before reading further, consider these points:

- What objectives might the teacher have in mind when her students engage in these activities?
- What level of complexity do these activities require?

Example 1: In order to create the described timeline, students would need to think about their project, take it apart by identifying what must be done to complete it, sequence the steps, and then estimate how time should be allocated to each of them. The process of taking apart something that is whole is the process of analysis. As students think about what they need to do in a sequential way to complete their project, they are learning to analyze a long-term task. The timeline is really a by-product of the analysis. We can expand upon the activity to create a lesson objective. The objective of the lesson might be this:

Students will engage in a task analysis in order to create an effective plan in order to create an effective plan for project completion.

The knowledge that students are gaining is best described as procedural knowledge, learning how to do task analysis.

Example 2: This activity uses the word *create,* but it is not on the highest level of the taxonomy. In order to determine the level of complexity, we should determine why the teacher might want her students to create such a timeline. One reason might be because she wants her students to remember these events, and the activity is intended to reinforce learning. Because most textbooks use text features such as headings and italics to draw students' attention to what is important, making a timeline using the text would not require students to think deeply when deciding what to include. A possible objective is this*:*

After creating a timeline of important historical events, students will remember the dates of those events and the sequence in which they occurred. Students are gaining factual knowledge.

Example 3: Because students are creating a timeline that will guide the development of an original short story, this activity is truly at the level, *create.* Each student's work will be unique and be reflected in the individual development of characters and plot. Students will need to understand how to write a short story, and how to develop voice as well as other aspects of the creative writing process. The timeline is an organizational tool to guide the development of their protagonist as they decide which life events influence his character and choices. The objective for the lesson might be the following:

Students will create a timeline of the significant events to guide the development of a protagonist for the short story that they are writing.

As they reflect on their own creative thinking, they are gaining both procedural and metacognitive knowledge.

Example 4: As students engage in this activity, they are not creating the events, nor are they simply placing them on a timeline. Rather, they are making a *judgment* regarding the significance of events based on specific criteria (impact on the national economy). In addition, they are required to explain why they believe that the event is one of the ten most significant. This activity asks students to *evaluate*. The objective might be this:

Students will evaluate the importance of historical events based on their impact on American economic development.

The knowledge that students are gaining is conceptual.

Here is a final tip on how you can determine the level of complexity of your lesson. After you complete your lesson plan, answer the lesson's aim question. If you find that the answer is factual, or that it does not require much thought, it will not engage your students in critical thinking. You will want to level it up. If you could not answer the question, based on the activities in the lesson and your students' prior knowledge, you need to revise the lesson.

METACOGNITIVE KNOWLEDGE

Before we conclude our chapter on critical thinking, we should also think about metacognitive knowledge, the new category of knowledge in the revised taxonomy. Teachers have incorporated metacognition into lessons, and researchers have examined its positive impact on teaching and learning for decades (Bransford, Brown, & Cocking, 1999; Weinstein & Mayer, 1986). The taxonomy defines metacognitive knowledge as knowledge of cognition in general as well as awareness and knowledge of one's own cognition (Krathwohl, 2002). Types of metacognition include strategies for learning, thinking, and problem solving. Students also engage in metacognition when they learn what, how, when, and why they use these strategies. They engage in metacognition when they gain self-knowledge as they make accurate assessments of their strengths and weaknesses (Pintrich, 2002).

In most cases, metacognitive knowledge is embedded within lessons rather than taught as a separate unit of study. The teacher, however, must explicitly identify the learning strategy for the students to build an awareness of the strategy and to connect it with the learning. As in all teaching strategies, the more the teacher consciously incorporates the strategy into the lesson, the more students benefit.

For example, when a mathematics teacher presents a verbal problem to the class, she can "think aloud" as she dissects the components of the problem, defines vocabulary, weighs the validity of possible approaches, and finally solves and validates her answer. The teacher explicitly demonstrates her cognitive processes as a model of metacognitive knowledge thus facilitating student learning (Pintrich, 2002). Writing about problem solving can be an effective student application. David Pugalee (2001) found that students exhibited metacognitive knowledge when they wrote about the processes used to solve math problems. The students' writing also gave teachers a perspective of students' understandings and misconceptions as they attempted various solutions to problems.

There are times when the teacher explicitly teaches metacognition, as when she teaches specific reading comprehension skills. In this case, a teacher is naming the strategy, demonstrating the strategy in context, thinking aloud to model the cognitive processes, and guiding the students as they initially practice the strategy in short, shared texts (Harvey & Goudvis, 2000). The third-grade literacy lesson in Chapter 2 provides an example of this type of lesson in that it teaches the comprehension strategy of making connections.

A Third-Grade ELA Lesson Using Semantic Webs: Using Organizational Strategies to Promote Metacognition

Determine or clarify the meaning of unknown and multiple-meaning words and phrases by using context clues, analyzing meaningful word parts, and consulting general and specialized reference materials, as appropriate.

National Governors Association, CCSS for ELA,
College and Career Readiness
Anchor Standards for Language #4, p. 25

Successful students…exercise a variety of strategies to understand the origins and meanings of new words, including analysis of word roots and the determination of word derivations.

Understanding University Success, p. 22

For third-grade students, the use of semantic webs relating new vocabulary words to parts of speech, synonyms, and antonyms resulted in a 40 percent difference in gains on a standardized vocabulary measure over the use of defining the word and using it in a sentence (Boulware-Gooden, Carreker, Thornhill, & Joshi, 2007). The deliberate expansion of general academic vocabulary is critical if ESL and SEL students are to be successful (Freeman & Freeman, 2009; Zweirs, 2008).

Vocabulary webs are useful in all grade levels across all curriculum areas. Rea and Mercuri (2006) suggest that such graphic organizers use fewer words than text, thus helping ELL students to participate in the higher level thinking required to create the web. As an example, we turn to *Class Clown* by Johanna Hurwitz (1987), a popular third-grade book. In the first chapter, Hurwitz uses the word *obstreperous* in a note that the teacher sends home to Lucas's parent. Third graders are not familiar with this word. Based on the sentence in the book, "I find that Lucas is very obstreperous in class," the teacher would initially elicit from the students the part of speech for *obstreperous*. The part of speech is always defined to reinforce the classification of words in grammar. Students can start to complete a vocabulary web (Figure 3.8) with the part of speech. Students will develop a "personalized" definition for *obstreperous* as they analyze the illustration on the front cover of *Class Clown* and the context of the first chapter.

The teacher then used a cooperative activity, Think-Pair-Share. Each student independently records one synonym with proof from the text and one antonym. The student then pairs with a partner to compare words, discuss agreement or disagreement, and finally share the words with the class. The teacher circulates during the

(Continued)

(Continued)

cooperative activity to monitor student work, correct misunderstandings, and keep students focused on the task. During the class share, the teacher records the input from the partners on the smart board for future use and reinforcement. Students add words to their web. The web now provides a student-generated definition for *obstreperous* based on illustrations and context clues. For homework, students write a sentence using the vocabulary word. These are shared during the next ELA lesson and added to the chart paper or the smart board.

Figure 3.8 Sample Vocabulary Web

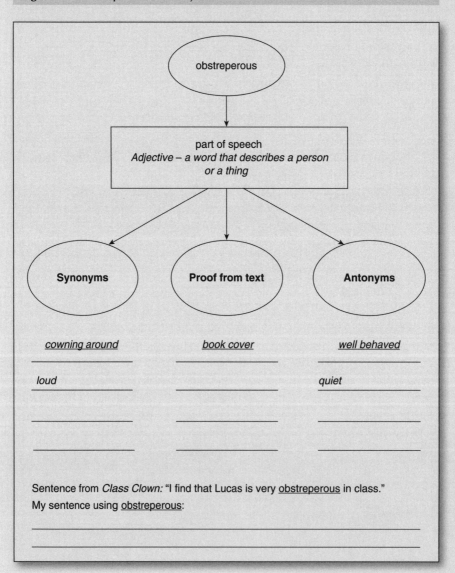

Sentence from *Class Clown:* "I find that Lucas is very <u>obstreperous</u> in class."
My sentence using <u>obstreperous</u>:

A Model Lesson: A Middle-Years Mathematics Lesson Using Self-Assessment

Mathematically proficient students check their answers to problems using a different method, and they continually ask themselves, "Does this make sense?" They can understand the approaches of others to solving complex problems and identify correspondences between different approaches.

National Governors Association, CCSS for Mathematics, p. 6

Problem solving involves analytic processes and sets of skills. These skills include:...taking risks and accepting failure as part of the learning process. When students do not find the correct answer to a problem, it is an opportunity to revisit the procedures they use, trying new ones and ask further questions.

Understanding University Success, p. 29

Assessments provide another application of metacognitive knowledge. Teachers often create review tools for their students prior to an exam and then require students to correct exam questions after the test. There are ways to use these activities to help students reflect on their own problem solving skills.

A teacher can design a series of "solved" problems that contain errors. Students must find the error, correct it, and then write an explanation of the original mistake and the correct line of reasoning. This activity expands general strategies for problem solving into a new arena of error analysis (Figure 3.9) which will then transfer so that students can better examine their own thinking and their own work. If the teacher includes anticipated error, which was discussed in Chapter 2, the review sheet is even more effective.

The second component of the assessment occurs after the examination. Self-knowledge is developed when students develop knowledge of their own strengths and weaknesses. Students can reflect and write about their performance on the test topics and evaluate the strategies they used to prepare for the exam. Test corrections, which mirror the review sheet, can then be used. The teacher provides the student with a three-column sheet. In the first column, the student copies the example

(Continued)

(Continued)

with the error; in the second, shows the correct solution; and in the third; writes an explanation of the error and why the solution in the second column is correct.

ELL teachers should explicitly teach their students both of these strategies. This metacognitive knowledge helps ELL students become aware of their thinking and their approach to solving problems; this builds a level of confidence in using specific strategies for future learning (Rea & Mercuri, 2006).

Figure 3.9 A Different Approach—You Be the Teacher

In each of the following problems, the student made a mistake. Determine the correct answer and explain the mistake made by the student.

Problem	Corrected	Explanation
Jerry's family farm measures 7 miles by 5 miles. Determine the area of the farm. $2 \times 7 + 2 \times 5 = 14 + 10$ answer is 24		
$5(x + 3) = 19 + x$ $5x + 3 = 19 + x$ $4x = 16$ $x = 4$		
$3 \times 2^3 = 216$		

STRATEGIES FOR INFUSING HIGHER LEVEL THINKING INTO LESSONS

Creating lessons that develop critical thinking skills along with content knowledge is not easy and takes practice. Below, we suggest strategies for developing lessons with cognitive complexity in mind. We use the taxonomy itself to do so!

Internalize the taxonomy until you **remember** it. Staple Figure 3.3 in your plan book or create your own "cheat sheet."

Understand the taxonomy by reading about it. We recommend the sources that are included as references in this chapter. Often we classify activities at a higher cognitive level than they actually are.

Apply your conceptual knowledge by creating objectives that reflect different levels of cognitive complexity. Ask a colleague at which level of complexity they would place the objectives that you create.

Analyze your lessons as we analyzed the lesson in this chapter—both by complexity and knowledge type.

After you have completed your analysis, **evaluate** the lesson. Ask the following questions:

- To what extent do the activities in the lesson allow all students to reach the level of complexity designed in the objective?
- Is it possible to build in additional higher level thinking?
- If in your judgment, there can be better alignment or additional opportunities for higher level thinking, **analyze** the lesson again.
- How can I bridge the gap by creating activities that are better aligned with the complexity of the objective? Should I consider adjusting the objective instead?
- Is difficulty getting in the way of complexity? If so, can I adjust the difficulty of the materials that I use? Can I differentiate the difficulty so I vary the challenge? (Remember the varied handouts used in the second lesson on feudalism!)

Create lessons and units that consciously build the critical thinking skills that our students need. Begin by transforming your tried and true lessons until you are confident in your skills.

Accelerating the learning of all students while building in critical thinking is no small task. It can only occur in classrooms that are distinguished by a culture of equity—where the strengths of each student are valued and each weakness is addressed. Such classrooms give all students the opportunity to learn at higher levels. Now that we have discussed the *A* and the *C* of ACES, we will explore the very important letter—*E*—which stands for equity.

4 Equity—The *E* in ACES

GIVING ALL STUDENTS THE OPPORTUNITY TO LEARN

Ensuring that all of our students have the opportunity to learn is what equitable schooling is all about. The term *Opportunity to Learn* (OTL) was first introduced by John B. Carroll in 1963 (Burstein, 1993). Its importance as a determinant of student achievement was recognized by the *First International Mathematics Survey*, which took place during the same era. *Opportunity to Learn* (OTL) represents a simple yet powerful concept—students cannot be expected to master what they have not been taught (Burstein, 1993; Lucas, 1999). Those who support OTL identify *curriculum* as a primary determinant of students' learning. In Linda Darling-Hammond's (2010) recent book on equity, she notes that decades of research show that student "access to curriculum opportunities is a more powerful determinant of achievement than initial achievement levels" (p. 54). Our own research confirms this as well (Burris & Garrity, 2009; Burris, Heubert, & Levin, 2006).

If the Common Core remains true to the spirit of *Opportunity to Learn*, and its focus is on standards that influence curriculum, we predict that it will be a great success and more students will indeed become college and career ready. If, however, the Core becomes the foundation for new testing that punishes students, teachers, and schools if scores do not increase, it will not bring equity, but rather greater inequities. We write this chapter and this book with a cautious optimism that giving all students access to enriched curriculum will be the primary focus of the Core's implementation.

Although the term, *Opportunity to Learn* was first used in 1963, equitable access to challenging curriculum is still very uneven. The latest data from the Civil Rights Data Collection survey of 2009–10 show disparities in OTL that are breathtaking despite decades of federal reforms. There are thousands of high schools that do not offer a mathematics class more challenging than Algebra I. Twenty percent of white students in Boston are enrolled in Advanced Placement courses, but the percentage drops to 8 percent for black and Latino students in the same city (Khadaroo, 2011).

Despite studies that clearly link challenging curriculum to successful college completion (Adelman, 1999), many students do not have access to the courses that they need for postsecondary success. The inequities among schools and the inequitable access to excellence within schools are two reasons why the *Opportunity to Learn* is out of reach for so many of our students.

Barriers to Equitable Schooling

As noted above, American schools are far from equal when it comes to providing excellent opportunities for learning. For example, the opportunity gap between white and Asian American students vs. black and Latino students persists as documented by the civil rights survey discussed above. The gap in opportunity is due to two critical barriers to equitable schooling—racial isolation and tracking.

Racially Isolated Schooling

Even though nearly sixty years have come and gone since *Brown v. the Board of Education* (1954), America's schools are becoming more, not less, segregated (Orfield & Lee, 2006). The harmfulness of racial segregation was widely understood in the 1970s, but the nation has shifted its focus to an "educate where they are" philosophy grounded in the notion that we can feign colorblindness and do just fine. We cannot. Separate but equal was not fine prior to *Brown v. the Board of Education* and it is not fine now. The disparities between urban schools with high concentrations of students from low socioeconomic (SES) households and suburban schools that serve upper middle class homes are well known. The fact that schools which have a higher proportion of minority or low SES students are less likely to offer challenging curriculum, such as AP courses, is but one example (Handerwork, Tognatta, Coley, & Gittomer, 2008). Policymakers must muster the courage to confront this most difficult issue of equity.

Tracking and Ability Grouping

Although a meaningful discussion of policies to reduce racial isolation in schooling is beyond the scope of this book (as well as beyond the control of individual schools), the second barrier to universal access to opportunity to learn is not. In the majority of America's middle and high schools, access to excellent learning opportunities is gated by tracking systems or ability grouping. Since the turn of the 20th century, schools have practiced tracking, or the differentiation of instruction, by placing students in different classes based on perceived ability (Kliebard, 1995; Oakes, 2005). Unfortunately, such grouping practices continue despite years of research that demonstrates the harm that tracking causes. We know from researcher Jeannie Oakes (2005) and others that tracking depresses student achievement and causes racial and socioeconomic stratification in schools (Braddock & Dawkins, 1993; Welner, 2001). There is also an extensive body of research which shows that even in schools that are racially integrated, the practice of tracking, or ability grouping, resegregates students within those schools (George, 1992; Oakes, 2005). Minority students are overrepresented in low-track classes and underrepresented in high-track classes, even after taking students' prior achievements into account (Mickelson, 2001; Slavin & Braddock, 1993; Welner, 2001). We also know that track assignment is influenced by factors unrelated to student achievement, giving advantage to the children of college educated parents (Useem, 1992).

If students are to meet the Common Core State Standards (CCSS), they need to learn the enriched, high-track curriculum generally reserved for high achievers. From both research and practice, we know that providing all students challenging learning experiences in heterogeneously grouped classes is the most effective and equitable way to bring all students to higher achievement (Burris & Garrity, 2009). The following section explains why heterogeneous, detracked classes are so important.

HOW DETRACKING PROMOTES BOTH EQUITY AND EXCELLENCE

Every classroom has a culture. If all students are to become college and career ready, they must work together in an environment that is challenging and enriched and where high expectations are held for all. Students learn from each other as well as from their teacher. If they are to participate in discussions that are rich in critical thinking, then students must be exposed to classmates who are intellectual risk takers and willing participants in high level discussions. Our Standard English learners (SELs) and English language learners (ELLs) must hear academic vocabulary used as part of classroom discourse if they are to develop the academic vocabulary that they need (Calderon & Minaya-Rowe, 2011; Zweirs, 2008). Likewise, students from upper middle class homes must hear the point of view of students who live with far fewer resources and have different life stories in order to develop an understanding of social justice and to appreciate literature that reflects a culture different from their own. Special education students must develop confidence and identity as learners outside of the sheltered environment of self-contained classrooms. All of the above happens best when the classroom reflects the diversity, in both achievement and culture, of a school.

Some argue that the struggling student is overwhelmed in such an environment, but that they can be leaders in a low-track class. They believe that the solution is to provide the same curriculum but to teach it at a slower pace. That is an interesting theory, but it is not borne out by research. Attempts to reform low-track classes have not met with success—in school after school, such classes are characterized by disproportionate numbers of minority students and students from low SES households, low expectations, behavior management issues, and the least qualified teachers (Oakes, 2005). In schools, the squeaky wheels get the best teachers, and the squeakiest wheels of all are the parents of high achievers.

For those who have only taught tracked classes, the transition can seem formidable and difficult to imagine. Certainly, meeting the needs of special education students, English language learners, and the most proficient learners all in the same classroom is a challenge. However, it can be accomplished with great success (Burris & Garrity, 2008; Garrity, 2004: Garrity & Burris, 2007). For more information on how to successfully detrack, we recommend our book, *Detracking for Excellence and Equity* (Burris & Garrity, 2008). In this chapter we will explain strategies and share effective lessons and ideas that can be implemented or adapted and refined for our readers' practice.

Despite our passion for equitable classrooms, we realize that although teachers can be advocates for detracking, ultimately such decisions are made at the district, not teacher level. Although the strategies that follow are designed for heterogeneous classes, they can be used in any class—after all, all classrooms are filled with students who are unique, and therefore to some extent, heterogeneous. Whether you teach in a heterogeneously grouped classroom (and we hope that you do) or one that is tracked, the strategies and lessons that we share in this chapter can foster equitable access to a challenging curriculum for students.

ACTIVELY ENGAGING ALL STUDENTS IN LEARNING

When we talk about how to allow all students access to high level learning, we always begin with the basics. The first basic principle is that learning occurs in the mind of the learner. As we discussed in Chapter 2, learners actively seek to make connections with prior experiences as they negotiate what they are learning with what they have learned before. All learners need time to retrieve information, to process new learning, to make meaning and connections that make new knowledge both useful and memorable, and to practice that learning to promote retention. What differs from learner to learner are the instructional conditions that they need to make learning happen. Our job as teachers is to provide access by creating lessons that are student-centered with ample opportunity for students to demonstrate understanding.

This is what effective differentiation is all about. Unlike those who believe in tracking, we stand firm in our belief that all students deserve to be taught the same excellent curriculum. What differs is *how* you teach it. Differentiation occurs in the methods we use to help different students learn the curriculum, not in the standards that we hold for them.

For example, students with learning disabilities in reading or who are emerging English language learners might require an audio and a written version of text. Students who have a limited academic vocabulary may need additional vocabulary supports during or outside of class. We may need to differentiate the *difficulty* level of the materials we use to deliver content. Well-organized chalk boards, with posted aim questions for the lesson, help students with attention deficit disorder (ADD) or organizational challenges to follow the lesson and record notes with minimal confusion.

Not every student must do every problem on a math practice sheet— different problems can be assigned to different students depending on their facility with the topic. Challenging problems that require students to extend what they know can be given to high achievers. Prepared cue cards with formulas or procedural models can be quietly passed to students who are struggling with their math problems. The next chapter on support, the *S* in ACES, will elaborate on strategies that can be used to provide access to high level learning for students within the classroom and in small classes, such as resource rooms, which are designed to provide mainstream support.

DIFFERENTIATED LESSONS

We have never met a student, no matter what her gifts or struggles, who did not enjoy thinking deeply about interesting ideas. As administrators, we have been in awe as we watched brilliant teachers engage children who are generally silent, passive learners. We listened as children who were generally disengaged or shy contributed deep, thoughtful insights to class discussions. Whenever that magic occurs, it is always because the teacher designed the lesson in a way that allows all learners to enter the classroom dialogue.

Wise teachers compensate for the deficits that impede learning. As Jeff Zweirs (2008) reminds us in *Building Academic Language*, "when ideas are transformed into speech, transmitted, and then turned back into ideas, some things are lost in translation" (p. 12). Often, a lack of academic language gets in the way. Students feel out of the game and passivity takes over. That is why it is imperative that we bring them into a rich, heterogeneous class where high level thinking is occurring and academic language is spoken. The following lesson, designed for a heterogeneous tenth-grade English class, is designed to do just that.

A Model Lesson: A Differentiated English Language Arts Lesson for High School Students

Analyze multiple interpretations of a story, drama, or poem (e.g., recorded or live production of a play or recorded novel or poetry), evaluating how each version interprets the source text.

National Governors Association,
CCSS Curriculum: Reading Standards for Literacy, p. 38

In college, students are required to think and analyze ideas across texts (Conley, 2003). In order to help students develop that ability, high school teachers will often ask their students to read two works of literature, recognize a controlling idea shared by both, and then write an essay or commentary using both works. For example, a novel or short story may be paired with a poem or with an essay that shares a common theme.

The differentiated lesson below is designed to precede the study of William Golding's *Lord of the Flies*, a novel often taught in high school. *Lord of the Flies* allows students to explore themes common to great literature such as the struggle between good and evil within the individual, the nature of man apart from society, and how man reacts when his survival is threatened. In Chapter 6, we will return to this lesson and show how it can be integrated into a wider unit of study.

The text that will be used in this lesson is a poem by W. D. Snodgrass (1987) entitled "After Experience Taught Me . . . ." Poetry offers a wonderful opportunity to teach our students how to closely read and analyze text. It also presents a unique opportunity for students to understand how form conveys meaning (Clark & Fifer, 1999). Because poems are by nature shorter than most works of literature, they can seem more accessible to SELs and ELLs. Poetry is a perfect vehicle for a differentiated lesson that promotes higher level thinking. Because it is meant to be heard as well as read, poetry offers an excellent opportunity to practice the CCSS above.

Background

The students in this heterogeneous tenth-grade class represent a wide range of student achievement. Three students have learning disabilities that restrict their ability to read, and two students are English language learners. There are also students who have extraordinarily strong academic vocabularies and reading skills while others struggle with below grade-level texts.

For this lesson, the teacher chose the poem, "After Experience Taught Me . . ." by W. D. Snodgrass. She chose it for several reasons. First, she could use the poem to introduce the theme of the tension between good and evil when survival is at stake. That is a theme she would develop with the class when reading *Lord of the Flies*. Second, although the poem would require higher level thinking skills for analysis, the vocabulary in the poem was accessible to students—sophisticated enough to help build academic vocabulary, but not so difficult as to serve as a barrier for her SEL and ELL students. Third, because she was cognizant of the CCSS, she knew that when students heard an audio version of the poem read by the author, they would understand how both the written text form and the recited form contributed to a deep understanding of the poem. Finally, she knew that her students would read *Beloved* by Toni Morrison in Grade 11. This poem would introduce the students to the use of multiple narrators. The eleventh-grade teacher could refer back to the poem to help accelerate student learning through transfer.

Rather than teach a whole class, teacher-directed lesson, she decided that she would create a differentiated lesson that would allow all students to engage in high level thinking and contribute to the analysis of the poem. She wrote this objective in her plan:

Students will analyze the poem "After Experience Taught Me . . ." and write a reflection on how listening to a poem while observing its structure can deepen a reader's understanding.

(Continued)

(Continued)

Because this was a constructivist lesson that would ask students to uncover the objective through their analysis, she did not write the objective on the board. Instead, she posted a simple **aim** question:

What can we learn about the role of structure by reading the poem, "After Experience Taught Me . . ." by W. D. Snodgrass?

The teacher thought about all of the learners in her class and how she could best use their gifts and talents so that they could be active participants. Her first concern was to make sure that her students for whom reading might be a barrier could actively contribute to the class. She decided that her English language learners and her students with reading disabilities could listen to the poem and focus their analysis on the poem's recitation. She searched for an expert recitation of the poem and found one online. The Poetry Foundation (www.poetryfoundation.org) had a podcast recitation of the poem by the author. She would borrow the school's iPads and headphones for the five students who would analyze the recitation. She made sure that the special education and ELL teachers had a copy of her plan and the poem ahead of time.

It was also important that her highest achievers be challenged by the lesson. She knew that they could read and interpret the poem independently, and therefore they could spend their time in deeper analysis. Finally, she recognized that the majority of the students in the class needed an assignment with more scaffolded support. The teacher decided that she would integrate academic vocabulary building in their assignment as well. The plan for the lesson was for students to work independently with tailored assignments. Students would then work in heterogeneous, cooperative groups of four, with each member making a unique contribution.

The tenth-grade English teacher and the ELL and special education teachers created the following chart for assigning work and group membership for the lesson:

While the class was copying the aim, the teachers (subject area and special education) put the chart (Figure 4.1) on the overhead projector and arranged materials in four piles, by letter, on a table. Students retrieved their materials and began working. Students independently worked on the task that corresponded with the letter that identified the row in which their name appeared. Students in Row A had iPads with the recording as well as a written version of the poem. Students in Row B

Figure 4.1 Chart for Assignments and Group Formation

	1	2	3	4	5
A	Ana Peron	Cheng Zao	Andy Weis	Patrice McKay	Arturo Perez
B	Linda Ames	Lania White	Pete Arthur	Jantel Williams	Rohit Patel
C	Amy Chung	Tomas Brown	Andy Greenberg	Walter Smith	Jenny McKay
D	Jasmeet Dura	Anna Rodriguez	Artie Swanson	Jamel Brown	Chris Peters

were given half of the poem's stanzas and the final stanza, while Row C students were given the other half and the final stanza. Although students were not told, these two halves represented two distinct narrators of the poem. Students in Row D were given the written version of the poem only.

Tasks were assigned, in a handout, as follows:

Group A:

Read the poem silently. Now listen to the poem's author read the poem as you read along silently.

Notice how the poet changes the tone of his voice.

Circle the words when a change begins.

Listen for a second time. Is there a pattern to the change?

Why do you think the author's voice changes?

What do you notice about the way he reads the final stanza?

Group B:

Read the poem silently twice. After the second reading:

Describe the mood of the poem.

Speculate who the speaker might be and what we know about him.

(Continued)

(Continued)

What are the meanings of the following words in the poem (you may give a synonym or phrase that could be substituted)?

vain

excepting

priority

endeavor

Does the final stanza startle you? If so, why?

Group C:

Read the poem silently twice. After the second reading:

Describe the mood of the poem.

Speculate who the speaker might be and what we know about him.

What are the meanings of the following words or expressions in the poem (you may give a synonym or phrase that could be substituted)?

facial mask

dawdling

remorseless

Did the poem startle you? If so, why? How does the final stanza connect with the rest of the poem?

Group D:

Read the poem at least twice.

How many narrators are there?

What do you believe to be the purpose of the final stanza? Rewrite that stanza in your own words, explaining its meaning.

This poem is an example of what is known as the confessional school of poetry. Confessional poets use their poetry to show the repressed feelings that often lie beneath what they show to others.

Which line(s) best represent a confessional style?

Students were given fifteen minutes to complete their assigned task. They then went to their jigsaw group (assigned by column number) to discuss their analysis.

Each group (1) discussed their responses to the task, (2) identified three questions they would like to ask the poet, and (3) explained why the author chose to write the poem with two narrators rather than one. The general education teacher and the special education teacher visited the groups, providing guidance and taking learning notes on any student misunderstandings and confusions. These would be addressed the following day.

After about ten minutes, the teacher reconvened the class. She played the podcast of the poem to the class, this time including a short explanatory introduction by the author. She led a whole class discussion that analyzed the poem, including a review of the identified vocabulary. The class ended with students writing a short reflection based on the aim question. She asked the class to focus their response on the connection between the physical structure of the poem and the author's reading.

As the students wrote, the content teacher and the special education inclusion teacher worked with students who needed help with the written response.

Reflections on the Lesson

Differentiated instruction is a constructivist approach to teaching and learning. It takes into account student differences in background knowledge, prior achievement, learning disabilities, interests, and talents. The goal of a differentiated lesson is the maximization of learning for each individual student in the class. Assignments may vary in levels of difficulty. Materials may be individualized. The teacher deliberately designs different *entry points* into the lesson to help students access the content.

The term *entry point* comes from Howard Gardner's (1993) work on multiple intelligences. He identified five entry points or pathways to learning a given topic based on the multiple intelligences of students. These points are summarized below:

1. Narrational—the teacher uses a story to engage students in the learning

2. Logical/quantitative—logic or numbers are used to develop understanding

3. Foundational—key words and definitions

4. Aesthetic—the use of musical and visual arts

5. Experiential—students physically manipulate objects and materials

According to Gardner, when a teacher includes multiple entry points, she expands the possibilities for student learning. For example, in the lesson above, the teacher used a narration of the poem to allow students to enter the lesson. At the end of the lesson, she played the recording for the entire class so that all could learn from the narrative experience.

In our opinion, the hallmark of a good differentiated lesson is that it is distinguished by more student talk than teacher talk, and by more student work than teacher work. Although the difficulty or complexity of the task may differ, *all* students contribute their knowledge so that the class and each student can achieve the learning objective.

That is exactly what occurred in this lesson. Group A students, who analyzed the voice of the poet, were able to confirm for the group that the author created two narrators for the poem, not just one. From their listening experience, they were able to explain who those narrators were. Thus, students who are often silent during a whole class lesson became important experts in their groups.

The high achievers of the class were challenged by the Group D assignment. They were required to analyze the poem absent the scaffolding that was provided to the other groups. Their knowledge was extended by introducing them to the school of poetry to which the poem belonged. When the teacher assigned projects later in the term, she would design a project that incorporated more poetry from the confessional school of poetry. She would allow her students to choose their project based on their interest.

Model Lesson: A Differentiated Mathematics Lesson for K–3 Students

Mathematically proficient students . . . are able to identify important quantities in practical situations and map their relationships using such tools as . . . graphs. . . .They can analyze those situations to draw conclusions.

National Governors Association, CCSS for Mathematics, p. 7

> Write informative/explanatory texts to examine and convey . . .
> information clearly and accurately through the effective selec-
> tion, organization, and analysis of content.
>
> National Governors Association, CCSS Curriculum:
> College and Career Readiness Anchor Standards for Writing, p. 18

Throughout the Common Core Standards in mathematics, from kindergarten through high school, students must be able to collect, organize, represent, and interpret data. Kindergartners learn to use numbers in context when they describe and compare items with a common measurable attribute. In middle school, students will use random sampling to draw inferences, and in high school students will interpret categorical and quantitative data (CCSS for Mathematics, pp.10, 50, 80). These mathematics skills and applications are also utilized in science and social studies. All students, specifically SEL and ELL students, must receive reading and writing instruction in each specific content area in order to succeed. Graphs are a common text feature in subject area textbooks. Mathematics lessons that develop a deep understanding of creating, reading, and interpreting data also develop a tool for learning subject matter through the specific writing genre of graphing (Calderon & Minaya-Rowe, 2011).

This differentiated lesson addresses mathematics standards for grades K–3 with each lesson expanding and applying the base knowledge of collecting and interpreting data and numeracy. The common theme of each component is that the teacher employs an experiential entry point for the lesson by using the students themselves as a living graph and the data or information focuses on the students themselves. Students fully engage in the lesson and easily make connections to the activities in each lesson, and thus retention is deepened. Students independently (Grades 2–3) or with their teacher (Grades K–1) will write sentences based on the data from the graph.

Although these activities can be used at any point in the school year, these self-awareness graphs, which show similarities and differences between a student and her peers, can be an excellent tool for helping students get acquainted in September. The added bonus is that a teacher will have beautiful bulletin boards filled with the most

(Continued)

(Continued)

important element in the classroom—the children themselves (Sullivan & O'Neil, 1980). Although the lesson can be used and developed in Grades K–3, teachers can expand them through the grade levels based on student interest and understanding.

This is the objective for each of the lessons:

Students will collect, organize, and represent data in graphical form and write an informative sentence describing an interpretation of the data. Students will label the graph with a title and variables.

Self-portraits K–1

Each student needs one sheet of construction paper and crayons. The size of the graph will depend upon the space in the classroom but usually three feet high by six feet wide will suffice for this initial activity.

Each student draws a self-portrait and writes his name on the paper. In kindergarten, some students may need writing assistance. When the portrait is completed, the children place their work on a large piece of paper. As each student places his portrait on the paper, the class counts aloud to determine the number of students in the class. When the graph is complete, each student stands and counts off to verify the number in the class. A sentence is generated and added to the class graph, "We have twenty-two students in our class."

A question is posed, "How many girls are in our class?" Students quickly see that the gender information cannot be easily determined from the first graph. The teacher returns the portraits to each child, and asks the girls in the class to form a line across the front of the room. The boys do the same. Boys and girls should be in two straight lines so the number of each can be compared. Girls count off and then the boys. There are nine girls and thirteen boys. Which group has more children? Which has fewer? The original bulletin board paper is labeled *boys* and *girls* on the left. Students now place their portraits in the proper row based on gender. Now the graph is sorted by one characteristic, gender. The teacher records the number of each on the graph. Additional sentences are written about the graph: "We have nine girls in our class." "We have thirteen boys in our class."

The teacher can extend the gender facts with deeper questions such as, "How do we know which group has more students or fewer students?" The answer to that question should be derived from both the graph and from comparing the numbers. The teacher then asks the class, "How many more boys do we have than girls?" and then follows up with "How did you get your answer?" This question develops the concept of addition and subtraction. Students will approach this question in many ways. Each response should be validated using both the graph and physically with the students.

Finally the class must decide on a title for the graph. In a sense, this is determining the main idea of the activity. The teacher asks each student to think of a title and share that with a partner. Each pair shares ideas and the class decides on the final title.

Birthdays K–3

Birthday celebrations bring joy to all classrooms. Why not link this excitement to mathematics? This activity introduces the format of a graph that has two variables—month of birthday and number of students per month. The materials can be simple or more creative depending upon the teacher. The design of a birthday graph requires a large piece of paper (approximately three feet high by three feet wide). Teachers precut a uniform-sized symbol for each birthday month, for example, a snowman for January, a heart for February, or more simply, a uniform-sized sticky note can be used. On the classroom floor, the teacher tapes twelve pieces of construction paper, each labeled with one month. This is the model for the living birthday graph.

In K–1, the teacher will prelabel each variable on the board paper, listing the months along the horizontal axis and numbers on the vertical axis. In Grades 2–3, the students usually are familiar with a graph and should be able to contribute this information for each axis. Each student writes her name and birthday on the month symbol or writes the name, month, and day on the sticky note.

The teacher calls students by month to add their symbol or sticky note to the graph. These students then form a queue in front of their month on a line that is taped to the floor. After all months are called, the teacher and students match the number of students standing in each month with the number of symbols on the paper graph as each

(Continued)

(Continued)

student counts off. The teacher poses the first question, "Which month has the most birthdays?" She follows up by asking, "How do we know that?" For K–1, it helps to have children join hands across the months so that the first person in each month is holding the hand of the other first person, the second with all seconds, and so on. This makes the answer to these questions clearer from the physical evidence. "How many students have a birthday in that month?" The answers are verified by counting.

Students return to their seats. Looking at the graph, students verify the answers to the same three questions. Now the answer to "How do we know which month has the most birthdays?" has additional information as students see the tallest column on the graph. "Can we tell which month has the least number of birthdays?" Again the teacher verifies the response by observing the graph and then counting. If a month has no birthdays, she can ask the students with that birthday month to stand. When no one stands, the concept of zero is reinforced.

Hopefully at least two months will have the same number of birthdays. Using June and December as an example, the teacher asks the students with birthdays in those two months to come to stand at their month. "Which month has more birthdays, fewer birthdays?" When the students reply that they are the same, they can prove this by counting the students standing and by counting the notes on the graph. The teacher introduces the concept and the word *equal*. For K–1, the teacher can continue with comparative questions in a similar manner, counting off each time to reinforce number concepts. The teacher records a statement with each piece of information gleaned from the graph. For example, "We have the most birthdays in February, and we have zero birthdays in October." "We have three students who have June birthdays and three students who have December birthdays. They are equal."

For kindergarten students, these activities also provide concrete practice with the standards that ask students to "count to tell the number of objects," "compare numbers," and "classify objects and count the number of objects in categories" (National Governors Association, CCSS for Mathematics, p. 10).

For Grades 1–3, the conversation extends to how many more and how many fewer. The solution comes initially from physically counting and comparing the students and then by using the graph. The teacher emphasizes that one column is taller or shorter than the other. For third grade and perhaps second grade, depending upon the student response, the questions are extended to include the concept of a fraction. "How many students are in our class? Twenty-two. How many students were born in July? Three. What part of the class was born in July? Three out of twenty-two or 3/22." Repeat these questions with each month. Compare the fractions for each month "recognizing that comparisons are valid only when the two fractions refer to the same whole" (National Governors Association, CCSS for Mathematics, p. 24). In this case the whole is the class.

Grade 2 students can work with a partner or a small group to write a sentence about their birthday graph. Each pair or group can write a draft sentence that the teacher checks for accuracy. The students then transcribe the sentence onto a sentence strip. These *fact* strips are added to the birthday bulletin board. The Common Core Writing Standards suggests that students in Grade 2 should be able to "recall information from experiences and other sources in order to answer a particular question through their writing" and "write informative/explanatory texts in which they introduce a topic" (National Governors Association, CCSS for ELA, p. 19). These standards are initially addressed through writing in the content area of mathematics based on the self-awareness graphs.

Grade 3 students can take this lesson to another level with sorting, recoding, and analyzing data using Figure 4.2. Based on the class birthday graph, each student completes the table by recording the number of students whose birthday is in a given month. As a homework assignment, the students complete the graph to include a title and labels for the variables and record their observations. The observations are shared the next day with a partner. The partners verify the validity of the sentences and make corrections as needed. The observations will be shared by each pair of students with the class as a whole, and each one will be verified using the graph and with the students themselves if needed. As in the Grade 2 lesson, these observations can be transcribed onto a sentence strip and displayed with the class graph.

As an extension in writing, students can use the sentence strips as a resource to write an informative paragraph to "convey ideas and information clearly" and "develop the topic with facts and details" (National Governors Association, CCSS for ELA, p. 20).

(Continued)

(Continued)

Figure 4.2 Birthday Graphs

My Study _____

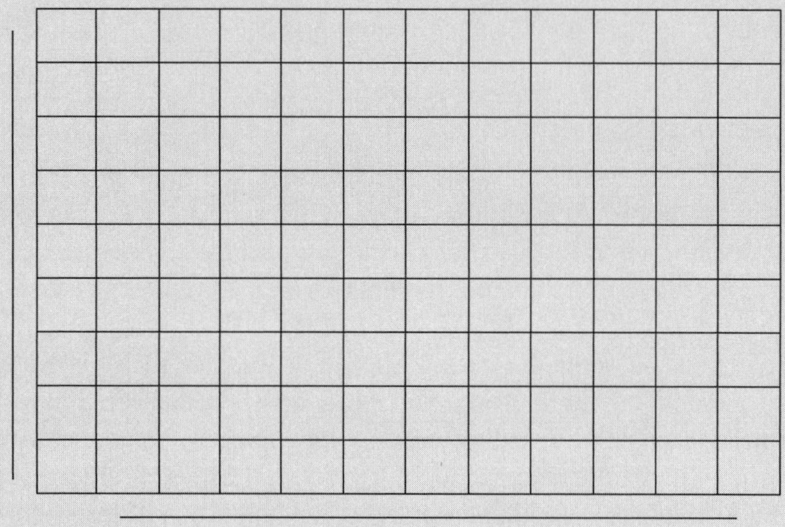

My Table

Month	Birthdays
Jan	
Feb	
Mar	
Apr	
May	
Jun	
Jul	
Aug	
Sep	
Oct	
Nov	
Dec	

Describe some patterns that you see.

Reflections on the Lesson

The lessons are a good example of how we can differentiate instruction by building on the multiple intelligences that our students have. The physical involvement of each student in creating a living graph becomes the means by which the class creates a paper graph, maximizing learning for each student. The teacher employed Howard Gardner's experiential entry point as students physically manipulated the learning materials. Additionally, the teacher focused on the bodily-kinesthetic intelligence from Gardner's work (1993) on multiple intelligences. However, she also incorporated linguistic intelligence, logical-mathematical intelligence, spatial/visual intelligence, and interpersonal and intrapersonal intelligences in the lesson. As noted in the reflections on the high school lesson, Gardner believed that students could be better served if educators presented instruction using a variety of intelligences. By blending the intelligences, the teacher helped students access the content and better understand the objective.

Students were fully engaged throughout this lesson with each student having a voice and taking part in creating the graphs. For special education, ELL, and SEL students, the creation of the living graph provided a physical and personal connection to the objective and both the living and paper graph provided a visual representation of the data to facilitate interpreting the data. The specific questions allowed these students to apply the data skills immediately and afforded the teacher the opportunity to check their understanding (Calderon & Minaya-Rowe, 2011).

The lesson incorporated a high level of student talk and participation rather than a teacher directed approach. All students contributed their knowledge and the teacher expanded her questions and reinforced the physical concrete model when appropriate, based on student needs. The teacher included how and why questions to challenge students and opened the writing part of the objective to allow for individual thinking and interpretation. All students achieved the objective.

The homework assignment for Grade 3, Figure 4.2, required each student to complete the graph from the table. The teacher provided an open-ended component by asking each student to describe patterns from the graph. Such a simple yet powerful item allows students to respond based on their level of understanding. The paired sharing and class sharing the following day provided all students with a rich conversation and insights from the graph.

The extension of the data to include the concept of a fractional part of a whole starts to build a solid foundation and understanding of the meaning of a fraction and the significance of the whole. Initially, students consider what is the total number of students born in June (three) and August (four) as seven students in total. When this is extended to what fractional part of the class was born in June and August, students begin to understand that when 3/22 is combined with 4/22, the result is 7/22 *not* 7/44, the all too common error.

The graphing lessons described above are samples using student data. Graphs can be added throughout the year to include eye color, hair color, favorite food, favorite color, and more. The self-awareness graphs provide a concrete and visual model for multiple purposes to reinforce a skill such as comparing numbers, to introduce a concept such as comparing fractions, or to revise a graph to include a scale. Each graph adds to the portrait of the class where each student views himself as part of the class but yet uniquely different.

A Model Lesson: A Differentiated Mathematics Lesson With Algebra Tiles for Middle School Students

Mathematically proficient students consider the available tools when solving a mathematical problem. These tools might include . . . concrete models . . . . Proficient students are sufficiently familiar with tools that are appropriate for their grade or course to make sound decisions about when each of these tools might be helpful, recognizing both the insights to be gained and the limitations.

National Governors Association,
CCSS for Mathematics, p. 7

Apply the properties of operations to generate equivalent expressions.

National Governors Association,
CCSS for Mathematics, p. 44

Apply properties of operations as strategies to add, subtract, factor, and expand linear expressions with rational coefficients.

National Governors Association,
CCSS for Mathematics, p. 49

Perform arithmetic operations on polynomials.

National Governors Association,
CCSS for Mathematics, p. 64

Middle school students use and apply the knowledge and understanding of arithmetical expressions during the fifth grade and beyond as they learn to read, write, and evaluate expressions in which a letter represents a number in an algebraic expression. Teachers must introduce this concept in a concrete manner prior to moving to the symbolic level. Algebra tiles are an effective instructional tool for this purpose. Algebra tiles provide a concrete model of integers and variables. They usually are two colors with green on one side, to represent a positive value, and red on the other side, to represent a negative value. Students develop a deeper understanding of the meaning of polynomials and operations with polynomials when they have the opportunity to use algebra tiles. These tiles let them see and touch the integers and variables that make up a polynomial so that they can easily transition to the symbolic form.

This differentiated lesson focuses on addition and subtraction of polynomials using algebra tiles. In Chapter 5, we include a support lesson using a visual model for multiplying polynomials. Too often when a student looks at $x + 2$ or $2x$ or x^2, they cannot describe the difference between each expression. However, if the student viewed a visual of each expression and can touch the concrete model of each one, the confusion usually disappears.

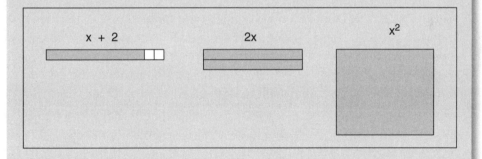

All students benefit from this initial development of the concept of adding and subtracting polynomials. Having this foundation will assist all students in applying the understanding in computational and problem solving situations. The algebra tiles help bridge the gap in understanding for struggling math students, special education students, and ELL students and SEL students who have difficulty accessing concepts through language alone.

(Continued)

(Continued)

The objective for the lesson is: *Students will be able to represent a polynomial in standard form and add and subtract polynomials.*

Prior to the class, the teacher created twenty-four small cards (half of a 3x5 card). On each of eight cards she wrote a unique second-degree monomial, all with the variable x to the second power, such as $-2x^2$. On another eight cards, she wrote a unique monomial, all with the variable x, such as 5x, and on the last group of eight cards, she wrote unique non-zero integers, such as -2. As students entered the room, she gave each student a card. The Do Now activity, verifying that students understand how to combine like terms, was on the board:

> Find other students with a term like yours. There will be eight in your group. Together, combine all of the like terms.

As the students found their like terms, the teacher circulated to listen to the group discussions, pose questions, and clarify any misunderstanding. The teacher asked each group to provide the final answer: $2x^2$ from one group, 3x from the second group, and 4 from the third group. The teacher asked students to recall the general name for each term, that is, monomial. She then showed $2x^2 + 3x$ and asked for the name of that term, binomial. She added, "Does anyone know any other word that begins with *bi-*?" Quickly students offered *bicycle* and *binoculars*. "What does a binomial have in common with a bicycle and binoculars?" she asked. Students easily discovered the common element of two. Finally she used the three terms as $2x^2 + 3x + 4$. Students offered the name of the term as trinomial. She followed the pattern and asked for any other word that begins with *tri*. Students gave the words *tricycle* and *trinity* and they linked the concept of three. The teacher presented an integrated web, Figure 4.3, to visually display each term and link them all as polynomials.

The teacher introduced each green (positive value) algebra tile—represented with light shading— as the integer 1, the term x, and the variable x^2. She displayed each on an overhead projector (OHP). She brought the students back to their class trinomial from the Do Now, $2x^2 + 3x + 4$. "Using the algebra tiles, let's represent each of your monomials that formed this trinomial. How might we do that? Think for a moment and share your thoughts with your partner." She invited one pair to display 4 on the OHP, a second pair to display 3x, and the third pair to display $2x^2$. After each pair set the display, she asked them to describe how they arrived at that configuration.

Figure 4.3 Web of Polynomials

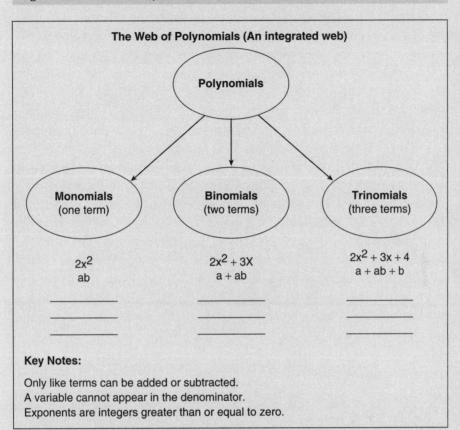

The Web of Polynomials (An integrated web)

Polynomials

Monomials
(one term)

Binomials
(two terms)

Trinomials
(three terms)

$2x^2$
ab

$2x^2 + 3X$
$a + ab$

$2x^2 + 3x + 4$
$a + ab + b$

Key Notes:

Only like terms can be added or subtracted.
A variable cannot appear in the denominator.
Exponents are integers greater than or equal to zero.

(Do Now cont.)

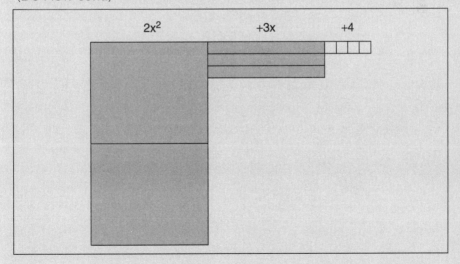

$2x^2$ $+3x$ $+4$

(Continued)

(Continued)

She followed this with a few more models to be sure that the students were comfortable with the meaning of each tile. She then introduced the negative model for each tile showing the students the red side of the tile—represented with dark shading—and comparing 4 in green with −4 in red, 3x in green with −3x in red, and $2x^2$ in green with $−2x^2$ in red. Using student sets of the tiles, each pair modeled three polynomials that were taken from the student text as model examples. Using the models from the students, the teacher noted the standard form of a polynomial, and students displayed their models in this form of decreasing degrees. The teacher modeled combining a positive 3 (green tile) and negative 4 (red tile) resulting in −1. She used the term *annihilate* to describe the process: when a green and red meet they annihilate each other, or in math terms, they *zero out*. The students like the annihilate metaphor much better! She modeled this with the x^2 tile and the x tile as well and then quickly showed a few more annihilations.

The teacher introduced adding polynomials using the model example from the student textbook.

Simplify $(3x^2 + 4x + 5) + (2x^2 − 3x + 1)$

Individual students displayed the model for each monomial in the two polynomials. Using the concept of addition as joining together like terms, the students, with prompting from the teacher, join the tiles $3x^2$ and $2x^2$ resulting in $5x^2$. Next, the combination of 4x (green positive tiles) with −3x (red negative tiles) resulted in x and the combining of the integers 5 and 1 resulted in 6. The addition was displayed in both horizontal and vertical form to give the students both visual representations. With a partner, the students completed a second addition example. The teacher monitored the students and offered assistance as needed. One pair presented the solution to the class using the tiles.

The teacher again used the model example from the textbook for subtracting polynomials.

Simplify $(2x^2 − 3x + 2) − (x^2 + 2x + 1)$

Students displayed each polynomial with the tiles. Using students' prior knowledge, the teacher reviewed subtracting integers as she posed the question, "When you subtract 3 − 4, how do you find the solution?"

Students stated that they add 3 and −4. She wrote the two expressions on the board. "When you subtract −3 − 2?" Students stated, based on the process learned in earlier grades, that they add −3 and −2, that is, they add the second number's opposite. Again the teacher wrote these two expressions on the board. The teacher asked for the proper mathematical word for the opposite of a number. After adequate think time, students offered suggestions and finally arrived at the term *additive inverse*. The teacher reinforced the word by asking the students to repeat the word three times after her. She returned to the two subtraction examples that were rewritten as addition examples and circled in red the 4 and −4 in the first example and the 2 and −2 in the second example. She wrote in red, *additive inverse*.

The teacher then applied this to the subtraction of the model problem for subtracting polynomials. "Let's look at the second polynomial, $(x^2 + 2x + 1)$. If we are subtracting that from the first polynomial, how can we add its opposite? Write down your thoughts." After an appropriate amount of think time, students offered the suggestion of adding the opposite of $(x^2 + 2x + 1)$ which is $(−x^2 − 2x − 1)$. Each of the green tiles for $(x^2 + 2x + 1)$ are now turned to red as the opposite is indicated $(−x^2 − 2x − 1)$. The teacher repeated the words and the flip of each tile and said, "'We are adding the opposite of x^2, we are adding the opposite of $2x$, and we are adding the opposite of 1." The students then combined the like terms and determined the answer of $x^2 − 5x + 3$.

Step 1. Show the original expression: $(2x^2 − 3x + 2) − (x^2 + 2x + 1)$.

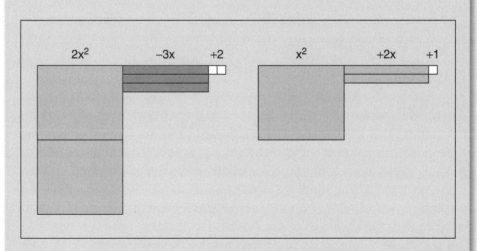

(Continued)

(Continued)

Step 2. Now apply the sign change for the additive inverse.

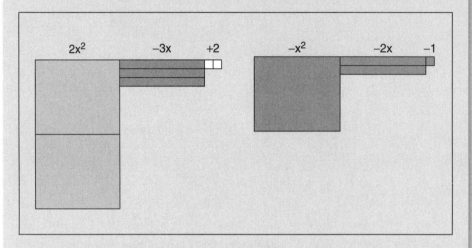

Step 3. Simplify or combine like terms by adding.

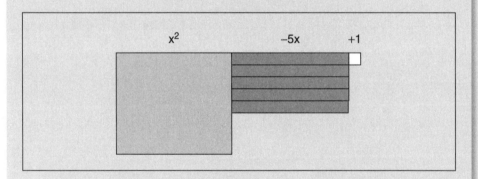

The teacher and students completed a second model in a similar manner.

For homework, the teacher selected four polynomials from the student text and the students were asked to draw tile pictures of the polynomials. Similarly the students completed exercises from the textbook on adding and subtracting polynomials. Students had the option of drawing the algebra tile representation. The teacher differentiated the specific exercises depending upon the student. All students completed a common set of adding and subtracting polynomials to assess understanding of the objective of the lesson. The teacher, however, provided some students with a set of tiles to use for the assignment along with some exercises on combining like terms and writing the final polynomial in standard form. Other students completed application of polynomial operations with geometry and word problems. The teacher offered an optional assignment of finding other familiar words that begin with the prefix of *mono-, bi-, tri-,* or *poly-*.

Reflections on the Lesson

Rather than use a sampling of five examples where students independently combine like terms, the teacher creatively assessed student understanding of the concept using an interactive Do Now engaging all students. She employed a number of Gardner's entry points: experiential as students physically combined like terms, logical/quantitative as students used their math skills, and foundational as the class defined the key terms for the lesson. The initial task for students was to find students with the same like term, clarifying what makes two terms alike. Students collectively used their math skills to arrive at a final answer. For ELL and SEL students, the review of the academic vocabulary for the lesson incorporated students' background knowledge and vocabulary knowledge giving meaning to each word (Zweirs, 2008). Further the integrated web for polynomials, Figure 4.3, helps students anchor the vocabulary and the concept for future use (Calderon & Minaya-Rowe, 2011). This web can also be used with the "words of a feather" strategy we will discuss in the next section (Zweirs, 2008). On the line between the words *polynomial* and *monomial*, the student might write the following:

A monomial is a polynomial with one term.

Likewise, between *polynomial* and *binomial,* a student might write this:

A binomial is a polynomial with two terms.

And finally between *polynomial* and *trinomial*:

A trinomial is a polynomial with three terms.

The algebra tiles provided a concrete visual model for adding and subtracting polynomials. Rather than following the procedural process used in the student text, the teacher used the same model problems but provided a bridge from the concrete to the symbolic procedural approach.

All students, both high achieving and struggling math students, benefit from this initial instruction to fully understand the operations in visual form. Many students struggle with subtracting polynomials as they try to understand distributing a –1 to each term in the subtrahend or being told to "change the signs of each term in the subtrahend and proceed as in addition." Yes, mathematically speaking, –1 is distributed to each term and you can follow the latter process; but does this really make sense to students without the visual component? This becomes another rote process with no understanding, thus limiting students from comprehending future problem applications using this skill. This web in Figure 4.3 and the algebra tiles will be used by ELL teachers, special education teachers, and math support teachers in their resource classes to reinforce the academic vocabulary as well as the concept and skills for adding and subtracting polynomials.

The lesson was student-centered throughout. The teacher consistently used Think-Pair-Share or small group analysis, thus inviting all students to partake in the class discussions and providing student-to-student discussion as an alternative opportunity to understand the objective. These instructional strategies provide the teacher with various means to assess that understanding.

WORDS OF A FEATHER—A SIMPLE DIFFERENTIATED TECHNIQUE TO BUILD ACADEMIC LANGUAGE

In his book *Building Academic Language*, Jeff Zweirs (2008) provides strategies on how to create visual organizers that allow students to link sophisticated content vocabulary together in order to learn the meaning of the words. One of those strategies is as follows. The teacher begins by placing related content words in circles or boxes on a paper. These become the "words of a feather that flock together" (p. 147). Lines are drawn between the words. On those lines, students create and write sentences that demonstrate that they understand the definition of, and relationship between, the two linked words.

Let's say for example, that elementary students are studying ancient Egypt. Their teacher wants to make sure that students understand the vocabulary for the unit. Some are academic words that are pertinent to the unit such as *hieroglyphics, pharaoh, papyrus,* and *pyramid*. She also chooses to highlight other academic words related to the unit that have broader usage—words such as *scribe* and *ancient*.

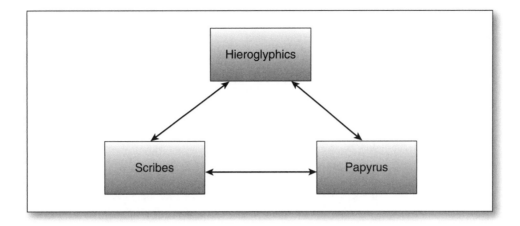

On the line between scribe and hieroglyphics, the student might write—

The scribes of Egypt wrote down history using hieroglyphics.

Between hieroglyphics and papyrus, she might write—

Hieroglyphics could be carved on stone or written on papyrus.

Between scribe and papyrus—

Scribes used papyrus as paper.

We can differentiate the task by adapting it to meet student needs. Struggling students who might have difficulty with the task can be given verb prompts such as the words *write* or *use*. Students who quickly complete their sentences can add additional sentences or enhance their sentences to form a paragraph.

Below in Figure 4.4 are four related words that played a prominent role in this chapter. Coauthor Burris used the above technique with these words during a staff development on differentiated learning.

The faculty who attended found it to be a helpful way to deepen their understanding. For Carol, it was a way to assess that the participating teachers understood the principles that they were teaching.

One of the participating teachers, Ann Landenberger, who teaches English at Leland and Gray High School in Vermont, immediately began creating sentences. She then created supporting sentences to form the following paragraph:

The only way we can get to true heterogeneous grouping in our schools is to advance the faculty in the field of informed and

Figure 4.4 Words of a Feather for Differentiation

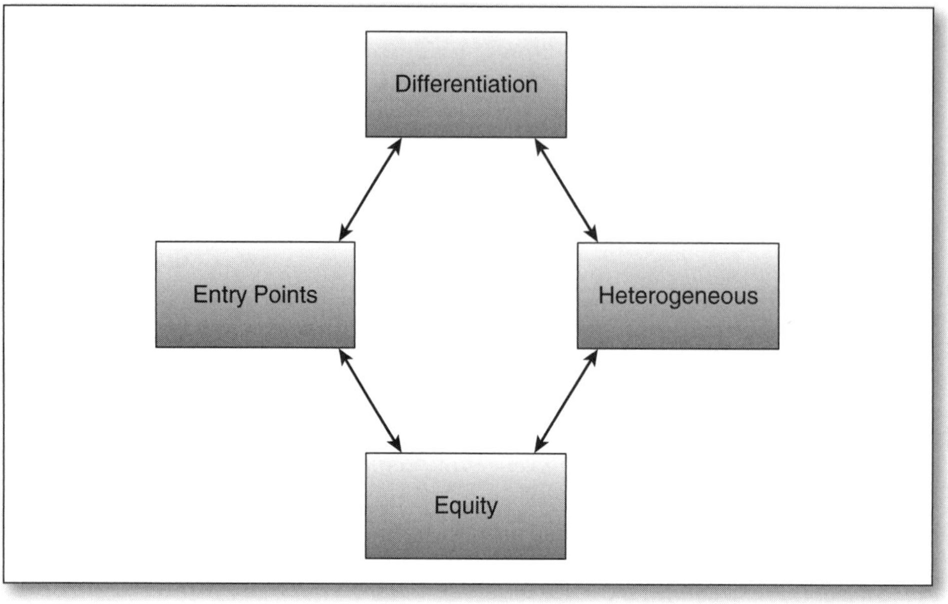

effective differentiation in all subjects, in all classrooms. Why should we care? Education may be the last salvageable vestige of true democracy. It has potential to be the ultimate equalizer and heterogeneous grouping ensures equity in education. Equity can be achieved through many channels, among them are entry points. We must grab the student early on in a period. Not at minute 62. The entry point for Joe will be different from Sarah's which will be different from Jesse's. Entry points are just one aspect of differentiation, but they are emblematic in that they establish first and foremost that each of us is coming from a different place.

Ann Landenberger, 2011

Annie, we could not have said it better!

WAYS TO INCLUDE DIFFERENTIATION IN ANY LESSONS

At times we will build lessons with a conscious effort to build in differentiated structures. At other times, we may need to use a more direct instructional approach and include differentiation in our presentation or questioning. Figure 4.5 provides what we believe are the most notable characteristics of a classroom that seeks to be a more equitable learning environment using differentiation.

Figure 4.5 Equitable, Differentiated Classrooms

Strategies for Equitable, Differentiated Classrooms

- The teacher believes that all students are capable of learning the content.
- The teacher encourages multiple student perspectives in class discussion.
- The teacher creates an atmosphere where errors are opportunities for learning.
- The teacher is cognizant of students who have an IEP or 504 plan, as well as students who are English language learners and Standard English learners.
- The teacher balances whole class instruction with individualized instruction and group work.
- The teacher thoughtfully prearranges cooperative group membership and monitors the progress of individuals and the group.
- The teacher assigns challenging extension activities to students who finish assigned tasks early.
- The teacher uses a variety of resources and materials and multiple modes of presentation based on the multiple intelligences of students.
- The teacher clearly articulates what successful student work looks like by using timelines for projects, rubrics, exemplars, etc.
- The teacher assigns cue cards or other scaffolded materials to students who are struggling.
- The teacher manipulates the difficulty level of materials and activities in order to provide access to higher level thinking and challenging learning objectives for all students.
- The teacher shares responsibility with coteachers or teaching assistants for classroom management of student behavior and routines.

CLOSING THOUGHTS ON EQUITABLE CLASSROOMS

Those who believe in the importance of the opportunity to learn must be vigilant and ensure that the college and career standards do not devolve into the college *or* career standards. Unless educators hold high expectations for all students and then tailor their instruction to meet the variety of student needs, we cannot achieve both excellence and equitable opportunity.

For school leaders, reduction in tracking systems that sort and select students is key. For teachers, lessons that invite all learners are the challenge and obligation.

Reflective Questions

As teachers create and examine lessons, the following questions should be considered:

- Are all students engaged throughout the lesson? Are reluctant learners given a voice? Are they held responsible for their classwork?

- Are multiple modalities used when I present information? Do I take into account the multiple intelligences that students possess?
- Are questions and problems tiered in a meaningful manner allowing ALL students to contribute to the discussion? Is there sufficient wait time after each question? Are questions asked on a variety of levels of Bloom's Taxonomy?
- Are there different kinds of opportunities for students to show what they know? Are all students expected to meet the learning objective? Do I account for student weaknesses and showcase student strengths?
- Is the lesson well organized with clear instructions so that all students know what they are to do? Is a minimum amount of time spent on organization? Are group membership or tasks assigned thoughtfully and quickly?
- Do I search for materials and examples that will appeal to my diverse students? Do I share my plans with the ELL teacher, special education teacher, or other support staff?
- Do I make sure that my most able learners are challenged? Do I make sure that each lesson has questions or an activity designed to meet their needs?

Creating an equitable classroom is a tall order and sometimes supports beyond the classroom must be used to help all students succeed. That is why *S*, which stands for support, is our last letter of ACES. The next chapter focuses on how we can support those students who most need our help in becoming college and career ready.

5 Support—The S in ACES

W alk into any yoga class and you will see some students using blocks to bring the floor up to them. The blocks compensate for short or tight hamstring muscles or legs that proportionally are just too long. Rather than have participants strain muscles or quit in frustration, the best yoga teachers encourage their students to use support. Their goal is to allow all of their students to engage in good practice and not allow barriers to get in the way.

If we are to prepare students for college and careers, they must fully participate in enriched instructional programs. Wise classroom teachers, like wise teachers of yoga, design support systems so that students who struggle are not left behind. They bring the floor up to them rather than keep students in basement floor classes.

Let's face it, for some students, initial instruction in the regular classroom is not enough for them to truly understand and apply the content of a given lesson. These students may need an alternative approach to master the objectives and to increase and deepen understanding. They may have a learning disability, or they may be an English language learner (ELL). Too often, however, educators jump to a remedial program and low-track classes to address student weaknesses, resulting in the students falling further behind (Heubert, 2002; Levin, 1988; Peterson, 1989). Struggling students need support to learn the accelerated and enriched curriculum that will give them the confidence and skills needed to be college and career ready (Garrity & Burris, 2007).

Our support model follows the tiered levels of Response to Intervention (RTI) in the 2004 reauthorization of the Individuals with Disabilities Education Improvement Act (IDEA). Tier 1 support or intervention begins in the regular education classroom; Tier 2 intensifies support using a smaller group in a separate support class or within the elementary classroom; and finally, Tier 3 provides the most intensive intervention via special education services in various settings. We believe in a model that is designed collaboratively by administrators, general and special education teachers, and subject specialists. It is founded on a rigorous curriculum with ongoing assessments to monitor student progress to inform instructional plans. We can teach students the rigorous curriculum that incorporates the Common Core State Standards (CCSS) (National Governors Association, 2010) if we design the *appropriate* RTI supports. That support, however, must be distinguished by both rigor and relevance.

Here is an example. Very often, our English language learners were poorly served. When they struggled, a teacher's only option was a referral to special education, resulting in the misidentification of some ELLs as having a learning disability (Echevarria & Hasbrouck, 2009). The RTI model has the potential to positively impact ELLs, as it requires early intervention using research-based, appropriate practices. Essential elements of RTI will increase the ELL's opportunity to learn:

- Setting high expectations for ELL students
- Ongoing targeted, professional learning for teachers
- Implementation of appropriate research-based instructional strategies
- Collaboration among the classroom teacher, the support teachers, the special education teacher, and the ELL specialist (Brown & Doolittle, 2008; Calderon & Minaya-Rowe, 2011; Echevarria & Hasbrouck, 2009; Vaughn, 2011)

In this chapter we will provide examples of how we can deliver the support that our ELLs, Standard English learners (SELs), and special education students need while retaining the rigor of college and career readiness.

SUPPORT IN THE REGULAR CLASSROOM: TIER 1

Response to Intervention (RTI) begins in the general education classroom where general education teachers incorporate Tier 1 strategies. Tier 1, which addresses the needs of all students, offers the most cost effective means to reduce the number of students who may need support beyond the classroom (Mellard & Johnson, 2008). Using the established curriculum, teachers regularly use common formal assessments and individual informal assessments to determine which students need support. The teacher then selects the research-based instructional techniques most appropriate for the needs of her students. As we discussed in the previous chapter, equitable access to the best curriculum demands that the needs of all students—general education students, ELLs, and special education students—be included in both planning and instruction. A successful inclusive classroom is one in which teachers create an environment where all students thrive both academically and socially. Following are effective strategies that can make that happen.

Cooperative Learning

> Comprehension and collaboration: Prepare for and participate effectively in a range of conversations and collaborations with diverse partners, building on others' ideas and expressing their own clearly and persuasively.
>
> National Governors Association,
> CCSS for English Language Arts, p. 64

Collaborative activities are a great way to meet both the Common Core anchor standard for collaboration while providing Tier 1 support. One of the simplest ways to begin to build in support is by developing a thoughtful seating chart. After getting to know her students well, the teacher carefully places each student in the room to support a variety of teaching models. Using a seating chart similar to Figure 5.1, the teacher places Lucas, who struggles academically, in the first row, first seat. Lucas is surrounded by higher achievers such as Mary, Peter, and Trish, who can work with Lucas in a pairing situation or in a group of four. This structure can be repeated throughout the chart thus allowing the teacher to quickly and effortlessly initiate cooperative work.

A teacher can easily engage students in cooperative learning activities such as a Think-Pair-Share or small cooperative group activity, knowing that each student will be paired in a supportive manner. Think-Pair-Share strategies can readily be integrated into any lessons. For example, when introducing the American Revolution, a teacher might ask an open-ended question, "Would the United States be better off under British rule?' Each student will think about the question, jot down some thoughts on paper, and share these with the preassigned partner (via the seating plan). Some pairs then share with the class at large. Struggling students have a built-in support system in

Figure 5.1 Seating Chart for Support of Struggling Students

Donald	Mickey	Diana	Chris	Ronnie
Fran	Delia	Bob	Carol	Buzz
Mary	Peter	Maura	Maria	Jasmine
Lucas →	Trish	Robert	Emily	Alex

a classroom where they can share thoughts and ideas in a nonthreatening environment, receive feedback from their partner, and develop the confidence to share with the entire class. During the sharing, the teacher can assist students, listen to the discussion, and plan the class share. The teacher can also take learning notes to assess who will need support during the unit. This also provides important information to help plan the unit.

Often, when students are required to do seatwork on their own, the struggling student quickly gives up. Partner work and cooperative groups can prevent such discouragement. Cooperative groups expand the setting from a pair to four students. When properly designed to promote both group and individual accountability, cooperative groups result in higher student achievement (Slavin, 1991). ELLs across all levels of English language acquisition can benefit from cooperative learning activities (Calderon & Minaya-Rowe, 2011). In the small cooperative group, ELLs and SELs will have a genuine reason to use academic vocabulary in an actual content area discussion (Haynes & Zacarian, 2010).

One of the drawbacks to cooperative learning is that it is easy for the most assertive students to take on all the work. That is why both individual and group accountability are so important. One strategy is for the teacher to assign each group member a number. The teacher can use the number to randomly select a student to present to the class. The group is responsible for making sure that each member is prepared and each member becomes accountable for the presentation. For example, teachers often create a review sheet prior an exam. Instead of each student completing the review independently, a teacher can assign each group one of the questions. After each group completes the task, one person from each group, chosen randomly by number, presents the response to the class. As in the prior cooperative experience, the teacher has the freedom to monitor each group, assess their learning, offer feedback, and provide instruction as needed.

Planning a lesson that uses these strategies takes time and care. The teacher must carefully create the content for the cooperative work, the individual and group accountability systems, roles, materials, and all other structures needed for student success. If done well, research has consistently shown that cooperative learning results in better learning and social outcomes for low, average, and higher achieving students (Slavin, 1991).

SUPPORT STRUCTURES AND LESSON DESIGN

Aim Questions

Struggling students often have difficulty organizing their learning. They quickly become overwhelmed and lose focus. Teachers can provide the support that they need by seamlessly integrating support structures into the lesson. Think about it. The few seconds that it takes to integrate such structures take nothing away from the more adept learner while helping those who need the support.

A simple and effective structural component for instruction is the identification and posting of the aim for each lesson. In their book, *Preventing Long-Term ELs,* Margarita Espino Calderon and Liliana Minaya-Rowe (2011) recommend this practice to middle school and high school teachers as an effective strategy for helping ELLs. From fourth grade through twelfth grade, students benefit from recording the date and the lesson aim in their notebooks followed by notes or model examples from the lesson.

Some teachers assign a number to each aim thus adding even more structure. When a teacher plans an assessment, she can provide the aim numbers or a list of topics based on the daily aim. Students can then review and study the sections of their notes when they prepare for the exam. Asking students to answer aim questions is an excellent informal assessment to determine which students are having difficulty. This can occur daily on exit cards or at the end of the week as a summative activity.

Cueing

Another structure that can provide support to the learner during the lesson is the use of cueing statements. Simple statements like "1–2–3, eyes on me," "write this down," "open your notebooks," or "class, look up at the board, please," can bring students, especially those with attention deficits, back into the lesson. Often students appear to be compliantly following the lesson but are not on task. The writing down of instructions for complex tasks helps as well. Directions for tasks can be written on a handout, overhead transparency, or on the board. The teacher can ask the class to read the directions silently and then call on students to tell the class in their own words what they need to do.

Cue cards are an extension of cueing statements. Cue cards are simply hints passed to students who are struggling as they work independently on a component of the lesson. For example, the class is asked to respond in writing to a quote. A cue card may have the definition of a challenging word from the quote or a clarification of the quote to serve as a sentence starter. Based on input from the ELL teacher, the classroom teacher may create a partially completed response in which the ELL would fill in the blanks (Diaz-Rico & Weed, 2002; Ovando, Collier, & Combs, 2003).

Scaffolding

> Students should be able to recognize information thematically. Doing so allows students to see the larger constructs inherent in the information and see the relationship between ideas and attended concepts and theories.
>
> *Understanding University Success,* p. 19

Teachers also routinely design scaffolding materials to present a visual representation of the content. The use of scaffolding allows the teacher to keep a task whole, while students learn and manage the parts (Clark & Graves, 2005). For example, in a third-grade class during a science lesson on simple machines, a teacher may design a framework or web to include the four types of simple machines. The center circle will indicate *Simple Machines.* Each of four spokes from the circle will be labeled: inclined plane, wheel and axle, pulley, and lever. Students could complete the visual as the lesson is taught to include a definition in their own words. For homework, the students will add an example for each type of simple machine and write a sentence on each spoke following the "words of a feather" strategy (Zweirs, 2008) introduced in Chapter 4.

We have found that this type of organizer and other types of organizing tools, such as the Cornell note taking strategies discussed in Chapter 2, present a structured note taking form that will help those students who struggle with organization. All students, including the most skilled, will benefit. As identified in the quote above, the ability to conceptually organize notes is a skill that is identified in the Knowledge and Skills for University Success (KSUS) (Conley, 2003) standards. We can begin to train students in this skill in the early elementary years by providing models so that students begin to see relationships and understand how to create organizational devices of their own.

The Response to Intervention (RTI) Tier 1 strategies discussed previously offer a variety of methods to differentiate lessons to meet the needs of struggling learners. When the classroom teacher, in cooperation with reading, special education, and ELL teachers, uses research-based strategies to ensure that all students have full access to the rich classroom curriculum, students can be successful without the more intensive RTI supports that are discussed later in the chapter.

Some may worry that the incorporation of RTI strategies will hold back high achievers. This is not the case. All students should internalize strategies that promote college and career readiness. For example, the use of cooperative learning might make students more comfortable seeking out college study groups. At the same time, students are learning invaluable skills for the workplace where teamwork is essential. Scaffolding materials like graphic organizers can be used in college and career to help create study guides, as well as organizational charts and task flow charts in business. In the 21st century, life-long, self-directed learning and communication skills are essential for success.

SUPPORT CLASS OR RESOURCE CENTER: TIER 2

Rigor and relevance go hand in hand. Support classes and resource centers take the rigor of the curriculum and provide additional instruction using alternative strategies. When the teaching team determines that a student needs more support than the interventions used in the regular classroom, a student moves to a Tier 2 RTI setting. Although there are many ways to provide support outside of the regular classroom, we recommend that support sessions be: (1) scheduled on a regular basis, (2) small enough in enrollment so that instruction can be individualized, and (3) taught by a teacher of the curriculum that is supported at the secondary level or taught by a reading or math specialist at the elementary level.

At the elementary level, some districts use a team model to support students in a challenging instructional program. The team may consist of a reading or mathematics specialist (Tier 2), an ELL teacher (Tier 2), and a special education teacher (Tier 3). Based on the needs of the students, all or parts of the team push-in to the regular classroom to provide small group instruction. The groups are fluid in that students and teachers move among groups to best serve all students in the class. The frequency and duration of this support will depend upon the intensity of the needed intervention. Planning is a critical feature of this support model. A common planning period during the school day or planning time before or after school on a weekly basis will suffice (Burris & Garrity, 2008). A classroom teacher may provide math instruction to the class prior to the team push-in to prepare the students for the follow-up small group work. In the area of reading, most teachers will utilize the team members for intensive reading instruction using a guided reading model.

Secondary Level

The following describes the model at the secondary level used in Rockville Centre Schools (Burris & Garrity, 2008). At the middle and high school level, a support class is a scheduled period in addition to a regularly scheduled academic class. The support class is specific to content. The most popular supports are in mathematics, English, and science. A heterogeneous academic class with full enrollment up to thirty students meets every day, and a support class of eight to ten students usually meets every other day on an odd/even or A/B day schedule. In nearly all cases, the teachers who teach the support class also teach the regular class curriculum. They may or may not have their own students. The teachers cooperatively plan for both the regular and support classes so that all students can benefit.

A critical component of a support class is that it must focus on the curriculum. A successful support class is not remedial in nature but rather complements and supports the instruction in the regular classroom (Oakes, 2005). The curriculum, that is, *what* is taught, is never differentiated. The instruction, that is, *how* the curriculum is taught, is differentiated in the support class. Teachers of support classes design lessons that teach the curriculum using an approach that differs from the regular classroom lesson to accommodate students' learning needs. The support lessons may present more background information on a topic, a scaffolding tool to facilitate a deeper understanding of academic vocabulary, manipulatives for concrete expression of a concept, or an alternative approach to the mainstream lesson. At times, student questions may guide or shape the lesson; however, each teacher must have a lesson plan that is both comprehensive and thoughtful. In the following section, we present sample support lessons in mathematics and English language arts.

Model Math 8 Support Lesson:
Using a Grid to Develop Multiplication of Two Binomials

Asking a student to understand something means asking a teacher to assess whether the student has understood it. But what does mathematical understanding look like? One hallmark of mathematical understanding is the ability to justify, in a way appropriate to the student's mathematical maturity, why a particular mathematical statement is true or where a mathematical rule comes from. There is a world of difference between a student who can summon a mnemonic device to expand a product such as $(a + b)(x + y)$ and a student who can explain where the mnemonic comes from. The student who can explain the rule understands the mathematics, and may have a better chance to succeed at a less familiar task such as expanding $(a + b + c)(x + y)$. Mathematical understanding and procedural skill are equally important, and both are assessable using mathematical tasks of sufficient richness.

National Governors Association,
CCSS for Mathematics, p. 3

Here is an example of a lesson in a middle school support class in mathematics. The purpose is to teach an alternative lesson after the initial instruction in the regular classroom. For example, regular classroom teachers present the multiplication of binomials using the FOIL method. Students use each letter to arrive at a product: *F*: multiply the two FIRST terms; *O*: multiply the two OUTER terms; *I*: multiply the two INNER terms; and *L*: multiply the two LAST terms in each binomial. If students can remember the meaning of FOIL and organize the results of each of the four multiplication operations, they will arrive at the correct product. However, students do not necessarily understand the meaning of each binomial as a factor with two parts, as this mechanical approach lacks depth and relies on a gimmick. Memorizing the mnemonic, FOIL, and the rote steps dictated by its meaning, are "activities that do not help ELLs" (Calderon & Minaya-Rowe, 2011).

An alternative lesson design using a two-by-two grid builds on prior knowledge of multiplying a monomial by a binomial and facilitates positive transfer. This visual representation will provide both meaning and a deeper understanding of the concept and thus increase retention. The integrated vocabulary web on polynomials, Figure 4.3 in Chapter 4, will reinforce the meaning of the terms and thus increase understanding of multiplying binomials by providing a visual model for ELLs and other students who struggle with language acquisition (Haynes & Zacarian, 2010).

The teacher begins with a prerequisite algebraic skill with which students are familiar. Independently, the students multiply a binomial by a monomial: 4x(x+4). Using student input, the teacher procedurally reviews the steps and solution and reviews the difference between a monomial and binomial. The teacher presents an alternative visual form (MathCamp, Inc., 2005) to solve the same example:

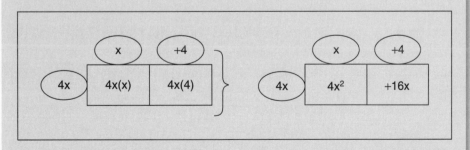

(Continued)

(Continued)

The teacher then poses an extension of the graphic for multiplying two binomials with the example (x+2)(x+4). Again with student input, the teacher thinks aloud to demonstrate how the box is expanded to accommodate binomials and together they complete each cell and the solution.

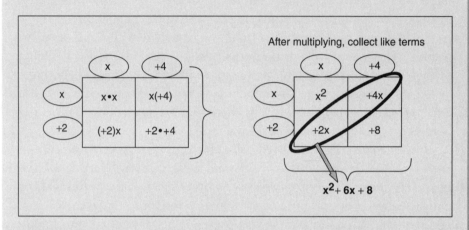

Following the same procedure, the teacher and students complete a second model, the difference of perfect squares.

An old favorite, what is the answer to $(x - 3)(x + 3)$?

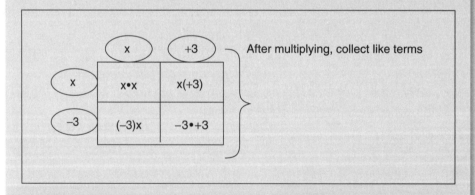

Usually the students do not need the first box after these examples and can move to using the final box in one step. Students independently complete a practice set with the box provided. (Figure 5.2). As an extension, offer students $(x^2 - 2x + 4)(x + 2)$. The teacher monitors each student's work and offers additional instruction as needed.

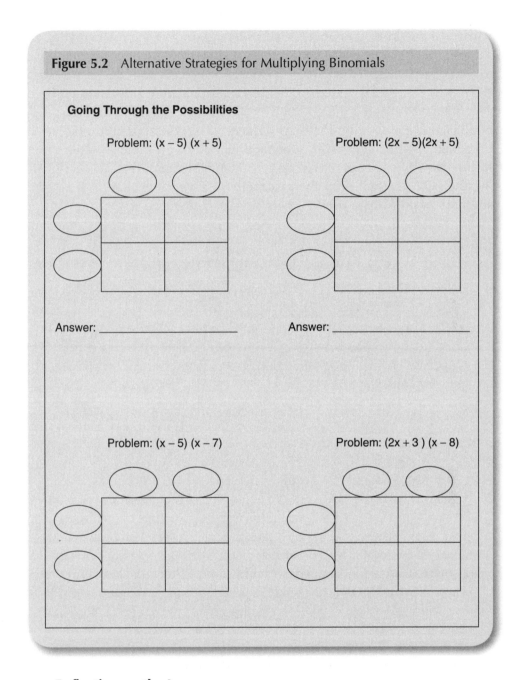

Figure 5.2 Alternative Strategies for Multiplying Binomials

Going Through the Possibilities

Problem: $(x - 5)\,(x + 5)$

Answer: _____

Problem: $(2x - 5)(2x + 5)$

Answer: _____

Problem: $(x - 5)\,(x - 7)$

Problem: $(2x + 3\,)\,(x - 8)$

Reflection on the Lesson

In this example, the support teacher offers her students a visual model for multiplying binomials. The think aloud during the first problem provided an effective method for developing ELLs' and SELs' content knowledge by describing the thinking process in conjunction with the visual model and solution (Alliance for Excellent Education, 2005).

Students will continue to use this grid when they need this skill or perhaps move to FOIL with a better understanding of the mathematics. In a support class, a teacher should not hesitate to offer extending activities to challenge the students. Natural connections come from this lesson, and the model can be expanded to include multiplication of a binomial by a polynomial by making the grid two by three and for multiplying two polynomials using a three-by-three grid. In each case, the student builds upon prior knowledge to deepen understanding and to promote retention. In a future class, the teacher may engage students in comparing and contrasting the FOIL method with the box method. This connection will aid the students when FOIL is used in their regular math class.

Model Lesson: High School ELA Support

Analyze the impact of the author's choices regarding how to develop and relate elements of a story or drama (e.g., where a story is set, how the action is ordered, how the characters are introduced and developed).

National Governors Association, CCSS for ELA, p. 38

In a high school English language arts support class, teachers can follow a similar format as the one presented above. The goal of the lesson is to support struggling students to successfully meet the objectives of the lesson or unit of study. For example, during a unit on Shakespeare's *Romeo and Juliet,* students in the regular class worked in differentiated tiered groups to examine the context, action, and language in Act 4. Students specifically would address the question why Shakespeare introduced a comic scene in Act 4 of the tragedy. The teacher will provide different support to each of the tiered groups based on the needs of the students. Some groups will be given the task as written. Another group may receive an organizer with the question, *Why did Shakespeare introduce a comic scene in Act 4 of the tragedy?* and a listing of the words *context, action,* and *language* in one column, a second column labeled *quote,* and a third column labeled *effect/impact on audience.* A third group may receive a similar organizer with an example of one of the parts: *action—Scene 4, Peter and the musicians trade humorous comments.* The students would complete the rest of the organizer with their group. Using this cooperative activity, the teacher has the opportunity to offer assistance to each group as needed.

Throughout the unit on *Romeo and Juliet,* the support teacher and the students create a timeline of the events in each of the acts. The timeline is posted on a side wall in the classroom. In preparation for the academic class lesson on comic relief in Act 4, the support teacher will complete the Act 4 timeline prior to the lesson. Students will work together to add either quotes or events for each scene. The teacher will engage the students in a compare/contrast activity based on the mood of each scene. Examining the tragic fatal events in this act, students will be able to identify the contrast between the comic relief and the tragedy.

Reflection on the Lesson

Together, the students and teacher have created a support structure, a timeline, to help students understand the sequence of the plot and the consequences of the actions and decisions made by the characters. The timeline continuously offers students an experiential entry point into *Romeo and Juliet* and taps the kinesthetic intelligence, thus increasing the level of student learning (Gardner, 1993). In addition, this visual tool affords students the opportunity to easily refer to past events in the play, to make comparisons, draw inferences, and support opinions. The compare/contrast activity requires students to analyze scenes raising the level of complexity for the timeline completion. The support teacher, however, does not include the why component of the academic lesson. That component will be the focus of the regular classroom. Rather, the teacher provides an opportunity for students to understand the events and plot of Act 4 so that they can fully participate in the academic lesson. Rigor and relevance are evident in this support lesson. The skill of how to create an effective timeline to help understand how plot unfolds is a skill that students can bring with them to college where they will encounter complex literature and have to understand it without intensive support.

Model Lesson: Elementary Reading Support—Grade 5

Determine central ideas or themes of a text and analyze their development; summarize the key supporting details and ideas.

National Governors Association,
CCSS for ELA, Anchor Standards for Reading,
College and Career Readiness #2, p. 10

(Continued)

(Continued)

> Successful students employ reading skills and strategies to understand literature. They make supported inferences and draw conclusions based on textual features, seeking such editing in text.
>
> *Understanding University Success,* p. 22

Earlier in this chapter, we described the ideal elementary team model for support. As a part of this model, a small-group reading lesson may be delivered in the regular classroom or in a resource center to introduce a skill or reinforce a class lesson. In this lesson, the reading teacher focuses on determining a *theme* in a story. This skill is often problematic for a struggling reader because there is an unstated idea embedded in the story (Robb, 2000). The student must use details from a story, reflect on them, and then make an inference to decide on a theme.

In this lesson, the reading teacher who is providing the Tier 2 support, employs a picture book by Barbara M. Joosse (1991), *Mama, Do You Love Me?* The choice of this book is twofold; first, the theme is somewhat obvious, and second, the setting is in the Arctic, a geographic region taught in Grade 5.

The teacher sets up chart paper naming the title, author, and illustrator. The teacher challenges the students to read between the lines today to determine the message or theme of the story. She begins the lesson by previewing the cover of the book. Students respond to the question, "What clues do you get about this story when you look at the cover?" The illustrations by Barbara Lavallee are beautifully presented with details of the clothing and terrain of the Arctic. The teacher divides the chart paper, as modeled below, into three columns with labels, *detail*, *prediction*, and *proof*. Students glean that the setting is in the Arctic. This is recorded on the chart paper in each column as "Book cover—Setting: Arctic—icy water, warm clothes, Inuit mask." (Figure 5.3) Now examining the title and cover of the book, students see a woman and a baby and surmise that they must be mother and child. Going deeper, the teacher asks the students to predict the answer to the question posed in the title. The children unanimously reply, *yes*! The teacher challenges them to offer proof for their yes. The students base the answer on connections with their own life. The teacher reminds the students to find proof in the story to affirm their prediction. Again student ideas are recorded on chart paper in three columns.

Figure 5.3 Organizer for Fifth-Grade Story

Title: *Mama, Do You Love Me?*

Author: *Barbara M. Joosse*

Illustrator: *Barbara Lavallee*

What is the author's message/theme? _____

_____

_____

Detail	Prediction	Proof
Book cover	*Setting-Arctic*	*Icy water*
		warm clothes
		Inuit mask
Characters		
mother		
daughter		

The teacher poses the question, "Where in the book might we find other clues to help us learn the author's message—what she wants the reader to know that is important?" She skillfully weaves into the question the teaching of the definition of the academic vocabulary term, *message*. Students suggest looking at the pictures and finding out more about the characters. The teacher begins reading the book aloud and reads it completely before asking for comments or questions. The teacher returns to the answer to the book title and students' suggestions to look at the characters and pictures to help with their task of determining the author's message or theme. She asks the class for proof that yes is the answer to the book's title question. Students offer many examples to show the mother's love for her child. As the students propose examples, the teacher requires that they record them on the chart. Students break the character line into mother and daughter and add examples from the story using both the text and the illustrations. She then asks students again to explain the author's message. Students suggest: all

(Continued)

(Continued)

mothers love their children, no matter how nasty a child is, even if her mother doesn't like what she did, her mother will always love her, mothers really love their children. In each case, the students presented proof from the story to support the statement. The teacher labeled the input from the students as dialogue, actions, interactions, conflict, problem, and decisions. These elements of a story supply the details from which the students can infer the message or theme (Robb, 2006).

Reflection on the Lesson

Although the reading level of this story is below fifth grade, the lesson incorporated the higher level reading skill of inference. The teacher did not want the students to get bogged down with comprehending the text; the objective was determining the theme, a relevant skill for fifth graders. Through the use of a simpler text rich in illustrations, the students' interest level was high and they were able to make inferences. The students clearly understood that through a series of questions and unusual what-if scenarios, the child in the book presses her mother to respond in each instance as to whether she would still love her. The mother expresses a variety of reactions but always affirms her love for her daughter.

The teacher structured the lesson and student thinking using the chart paper. The model develops metacognitive knowledge, namely, strategic knowledge of how to extract meaning from text and illustrations. As students, especially ELLs and SELs, internalize the strategy and make connections between the elements, the result is deeper processing and better comprehension and learning (Calderon & Minaya-Rowe, 2011; Pintrich, 2002).

The book preview, which used the book cover, piqued student interest and introduced the use of prediction and inference. The teacher used a picture rather than words to introduce the task of inference that the students would use to determine the theme of the story. The teacher explicitly taught the use of the text feature, the book cover, as a tool to increase comprehension. ELLs can use this visual in conjunction with their prior experiences with the relationship of a mother and child to begin to understand the higher level reading skills of inference and prediction (Calderon & Minaya-Rowe, 2011). Moving forward from the story, the teacher can expand the instruction to social studies by rereading the story to discuss the vocabulary unique to the Arctic region—puffin, ptarmigan, and lemming—and also carefully examining the illustrations to glean more information about the people, climate, and geography of the Arctic region.

In future lessons on theme, the teacher would use a higher level text and focus on one element at a time, for example, dialogue between characters. The model from the chart paper would be given to each student for note taking allowing the child to practice thinking and writing about elements of the text in his own words (Robb, 2006).

SUPPORT FOR SPECIAL EDUCATION STUDENTS: TIER 3

> Students with disabilities—students eligible under the Individuals with Disabilities Education Act (IDEA)—must be challenged to excel within the general curriculum and be prepared for success in their post-school lives, including college and/or careers. These common standards provide an historic opportunity to improve access to rigorous academic content standards for students with disabilities. The continued development of understanding about research-based instructional practices and a focus on their effective implementation will help improve access to mathematics and English language arts (ELA) standards for all students, including those with disabilities.
>
> National Governors Association,
> CCSS, Application to Students with Disabilities

Based on the evaluation of the on-going assessments in both the regular classroom and the support program, students are recommended and evaluated for special education services, Tier 3 of RTI. The level of special education services is determined by a Committee on Special Education (CSE). Collaboration and cooperation among general education, support, ELL, and special education teachers are essential to optimize student success when a student is classified within the special education program. The special education student continues to attend his regular education class and, in some cases, the support class, or ELL resource class as well. However, additional intervention is provided through an inclusion model or a resource room. This is very different from the special education, self-contained model which we believe should only be used for students with profound learning disabilities or developmental delays who need a life skills program. When self-contained classrooms are used to provide a watered-down version of the same curriculum, we believe that students fall further behind and will never achieve learning standards at the level that the authors of the CCSS expect.

Inclusion Support for Special Education Students

If the regular class contains special education students whose Individualized Education Program (IEP) mandates a coteacher or a paraprofessional, it is important to develop a clear role for each educator in the room. The special education teacher or teaching assistant offers the general education teacher another set of eyes and hands to interact with the learner and to monitor that learning. In addition, they provide a valuable role as they offer feedback to the teacher to adjust instruction accordingly. When a school initiates a coteaching model or the inclusion of paraprofessionals in the classroom, we recommend professional development workshops and the development of a protocol that coordinates the effort by the educators in the classroom. Too often the special educator is unsure of her responsibilities and spends most of the class time watching the general education teacher—waiting for cues from her colleague.

One strategy that we have found to be effective is the incorporation of field learning notes. This practice is loosely based on the Japanese practice of lesson study (Chokshi & Fernandez, 2005). During lesson study, observing teachers focus on student work in order to ascertain if the learning has occurred. The design of the lesson is then tweaked and retaught to another group of students.

This model can be adapted for use in the inclusion class. Based on the observation of learning, the second educator in the room can cue the teacher to student confusion by asking questions, reframing statements, or asking for additional time for students to complete an assignment. She can share the notes with the coteacher to let her know where students struggled and where gaps will need to be filled in the next lesson. Most importantly, she can gain valuable information on what postteaching or alternative teaching needs to take place when she meets with the special education students in the resource class. If there is a phrase that captures this strategy, it would be *eyes on the learner.*

Support in the Special Education Resource Room

Students who have an IEP based on a decision by a district special education committee may receive support in a resource room staffed with a special education teacher. A resource room, like a general education support class, provides an alternative lesson with alternative teaching strategies and materials but also must meet the goals of the student's IEP. The lesson complements the instruction in the general education class, thus better enabling the special education student to achieve the objectives of the rigorous general education curriculum. We must emphasize that the curriculum is not differentiated, as this would cause gaps in learning for the student. Rather the instruction is differentiated to provide strategies, often based on student IEP learning goals, so that the special education student can successfully master the curriculum.

Lessons may include specific content from the mainstream class when the teacher or teaching assistant notes that a concept or skill was misunderstood or not learned. (Remember those learning notes!) Let's go back to our support class lesson on binomials and look at a lesson designed for a resource room class.

Tier 3—Middle School Mathematics

For the middle school mathematics lesson on multiplying binomials, the resource room teacher might teach both the FOIL method and the box method, but include color to better illustrate each strategy. The teacher would assess which students are more comfortable with which method and ensure understanding to promote positive transfer of the skill in future applications. The teacher may also employ an integrated web organizer to reinforce the essential vocabulary—monomial, binomial, and polynomial—included in Chapter 4, Figure 4.3.

Tier 3—High School English

Mindful that some of her students have disabilities that interfere with their ability to read, and to support the high school English lesson on *Romeo and Juliet*, the resource room teacher could use a video clip of Act 4, Scenes 4 and 5, to develop note taking skills by taking notes on the comical language and actions in these scenes. The teacher will include a graphic organizer to structure the note taking. They will discuss what they learned in class about why Shakespeare uses comic relief in his plays.

Model Lesson: Reading the Science Textbook

By reading texts in history/social studies, science, and other disciplines, students build a foundation of knowledge in these fields that will also give them the background to be better readers in all content areas. Students can only gain this foundation when the curriculum is intentionally and coherently structured to develop rich content knowledge within and across grades. Students also acquire the habits of reading independently and closely, which are essential to their future success.

National Governors Association,
CCSS for ELA, Anchor Standards for Reading,
College and Career Readiness Note, p. 10

(Continued)

(Continued)

> First, successful students comprehend what they read . . . This comprehension of scientific literature with some technical language, content or concept is useful when students try to explain processes used to test a scientific hypothesis.
>
> *Understanding University Success*, p. 40

All teachers, not just teachers of English language arts, are literacy teachers who are responsible for teaching reading and writing in each content area. This is a core principle of the CCSS, which has literacy standards across the curriculum. Teachers must explicitly teach students how to read and use a textbook, rather than simply ask them to read a chapter and answer questions. In the case of students receiving Tier 3 services, we find that reading goals frequently appear on a student's IEP. A resource room teacher can address these goals by utilizing the textbooks the students use in the mainstream class to teach comprehension strategies and research skills.

Nonfiction text features scaffold the information in a textbook for students in order to prepare students for reading the text. The key element is that student must be aware of the text features and understand how to apply them when reading text and answering questions. In their book, *Preventing Long-Term ELs,* Margarita Espino Calderon and Liliana Minaya-Rowe (2011) identify teaching students to understand text features as an effective literacy strategy for ELLs. The same techniques are invaluable for students with IEPs who struggle with reading or with standard usage of English. Students must be instructed on how to use organizational features in any textbook, such as the table of contents, index, glossary, and appendices. These features assist students when they are scanning to find information on a given topic for review or research.

One of the more interesting and motivating ways that we can teach these organizational tools is by a scavenger hunt. When a textbook is introduced, the resource room teacher can ask students to find the title and subtitles for Chapter 3, the page number for information on ecology, the definition of ecosystem, and other information. She can expand these organizational features in lessons that include other text features. In each chapter, students should be taught to pay attention to print features, graphic aids, and illustrations; these elements signal importance and help students sort important and less important information. Each of these features are red flags alerting the students to pay attention—read this closely (Harvey & Goudvis, 2000).

Having a student master the use of each of these text features is a resource room lesson. When students start a chapter or section in a textbook, a resource room teacher can use a graphic organizer to help students organize each component (Figure 5.4). The organizer serves a dual purpose: it is a means to structure information, facts, and concepts garnered from the text, and then as a tool for review prior to an assessment.

Let's start with print features. In a unit on ecology, the first feature is the chapter heading in a larger font and bold print. "The Environment", the subheading for the section of study, again in bold print and a larger font than the regular text, follows the introduction to the unit. Students write these items on Figure 5.4. The teacher would identify or ask students to find the section of the textbook where chapters and subheadings are listed. Thus the students locate the table of contents. Next, she might focus on bold-faced words. These are the vocabulary words for the section. Students are taught to read the definition and read around the definition for additional information to deepen their understanding. Students also rephrase the definition in their own words or give an example to show further understanding of the academic vocabulary. Students record the vocabulary information on Figure 5.4. The teacher would identify or ask students to find the section of the textbook where definitions of words may be found. Students locate the glossary. The teacher asks the students to compare the definitions in the chapter text and the glossary. Usually they are identical. The teacher asks student how they might acquire more information beyond what the glossary offers. The students are instructed not only to look for the definition but also to *read around* the definition for examples and more information. Some glossaries reference a page number in the text. If this is the case, then students should be encouraged to go to that page for a better understanding of a vocabulary word. If the glossary does not have a page number or if a student wants to locate information on the term *ecosystem*, students are directed to the index. If there are multiple page references under ecosystem, such as marine, ocean, ponds, and so forth, the teacher thinks aloud with the students to determine which page would be used.

(Continued)

(Continued)

In a follow-up lesson, the resource room teacher could teach students the importance of looking at the captions, any graphic aids, or illustrations. Students should be encouraged to make connections to the content and what they know, because this enhances positive transfer to build new understandings. Again, students record these findings on Figure 5.4. In some cases when students analyze these features along with the print features, they grasp the meaning of the section. It is important, however, that students read the text after the review of the text features and completion of the organizer. They will find the text easier to comprehend and understand the information more deeply. The organizer serves as a tool for background knowledge and for reviewing for a test. In a future lesson, after students internalize how to identify text features and apply them, the teacher may ask students to alternatively read and answer the questions at the end of the next section without examining the text features. This will help develop the reading fluency required by KSUS and CCSS.

Figure 5.4

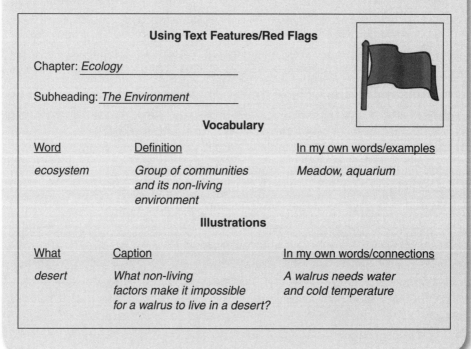

Using Text Features/Red Flags

Chapter: *Ecology*

Subheading: *The Environment*

Vocabulary

Word	Definition	In my own words/examples
ecosystem	Group of communities and its non-living environment	Meadow, aquarium

Illustrations

What	Caption	In my own words/connections
desert	What non-living factors make it impossible for a walrus to live in a desert?	A walrus needs water and cold temperature

Reflection on the Lesson

Effective use of the elements of the textbook should be reviewed and applied on a regular basis to reinforce the power of the text features. The applications go beyond the textbook to any informational piece of text: newspaper articles, political cartoons, magazine articles, trade books, nonfiction chapter and picture books, autobiography, and biography as a sampling. Even state exams often include text features in their questions. If students develop a level of comfort with text features and use them prior to, during, and after reading, they will improve their comprehension by being better equipped to construct meaning and understanding (Robb, 2003).

Model Lesson: Using WINK Sheets for Topic Review in Grade 5 Social Studies

> Students should be able to describe how their current place in time is influenced by the past and informs their future.
>
> *Understanding University Success*, p. 40

WINK stands for "**W**hat **I** **N**eed to **K**now." This organizer can be used independently by students from Grades 3–12. WINK sheets can be used by students for many purposes including personalizing academic vocabulary, detailing procedural steps in a solution, model examples in mathematics, and topic review for any exam (MathCamp, Inc., 2006).

Figure 5.5 is a sample WINK sheet for fifth-grade social studies dedicated to the three branches of the federal government. A resource room teacher might use this as a summary after an initial lesson in the regular classroom. Students complete the title of the WINK sheet based on a group discussion in the resource room. The teacher would display the sheet on an overhead projector, a smart board, or a document reader. As the students offer input, the teacher would record their suggestions on the displayed WINK sheet as students record answers on their own WINK sheets.

Students should work independently on the question below the graphic. Based on the response from the students, the teacher will be able to determine if the students understand the division of power within the government, as well as the motivation of the founding

(Continued)

(Continued)

fathers—to protect future generations from tyranny. The concept of checks and balances can be added to the WINK as an extension of this topic.

Figure 5.5 WINK Sheet

What I Need To Know About: _the three branches of the federal government_

Term	Example/Description	Example/Description
Executive	Who?	Powers?
Legislative	Who?	Powers?
Judicial	Who?	Powers?

Why did our Founding Fathers divide the government into three branches?

Reflection on the Lesson

This lesson complements the initial classroom instruction and provides a scaffolding tool to aid in student retention. Furthermore, the teacher assesses conceptual understanding with the last question. This extension increases the level of difficulty of the lesson because students apply the facts in the organizer and use critical thinking to determine the significance of this in the development of the US Constitution. Because the sheet is simple to create, by twelfth grade, students should create such organizers by themselves. This is valuable skill to help our special education students become college and career ready.

CLOSING THOUGHTS ON SUPPORT

To be prepared for the challenges of the 21st century, all students must be prepared to choose college or career. That means that students must be full participants in a rigorous, high quality educational program from the start of their educational experience through the awarding of their diploma. When teachers describe students who do not have the prerequisite skills to be successful in such a program, it is the job of the teacher to provide the support needed for that student to participate and succeed. The lessons and strategies presented in this chapter offer starting points for designing a strong support model in your district. Remember, when rigor and relevance go hand in hand, all students reap the benefits.

Reflective Questions on Support

As you think about your most rigorous instructional program, consider the following questions in terms of supporting that program:

- Do I incorporate cooperative learning activities into my lessons?
- Does the seating arrangement in my classroom lend itself to cooperative learning and student support?
- Do I cue students to keep them on task and involved in the lesson?
- Do I use the other educational professionals in the room to support student learning and give me the feedback that I need to know to determine if my students are learning?
- Do I teach reading and writing skills in all content areas (elementary) or in my content area (secondary)?
- Do I explicitly teach academic vocabulary before, during, and after a unit of study to accelerate English learning for my ELLs and SELs?
- Do I use scaffolding materials to assist my students in breaking a concept into manageable parts to better understand the whole?
- Do I include concrete or pictorial representations of content as part of my introduction to a concept or skill?
- Do I communicate and plan with the support, ELL, and special education personnel who work with my students?
- As a support, ELL, or special education teacher, do I plan rigorous and relevant lessons that complement the classroom instruction?

6 Using ACES to Build Learning

At this point, you may be feeling a bit confused as you attempt to classify learning activities among the four ACES. You may have noticed that many of the support (*S*) strategies could have been included in the chapter on equity (*E*). Critical thinking (*C*) promotes accelerated learning (*A*) when it gives all students access to a more enriched learning environment. The infusion of higher level critical thinking questions and activities (*C*) also makes the lesson more equitable (*E*) for students who are ready for a greater level of challenge.

Here are some concrete examples from the lessons in this book. The accelerated learning strategy (*A*) of transfer was deliberately used as the Do Now activity (*Write a list of four words or ideas that come to mind when you hear the word feudalism*) for the lesson in Chapter 3 on feudalism. This was a lesson designed to build critical thinking skills (*C*). The support (*S*) of listening to a recorded version of the poem in Chapter 4 made the classroom more equitable (*E*) for its English language learners (ELLs), and it allowed them to contribute their critical thinking abilities (*C*) to the work of the group.

If you weren't confused before, you may be now! Not only is confusion warranted, it is a very good sign. It indicates that you are seeing the overlap and connections among the four ACES. The ACES are natural allies. When they are used together, they create a synergy that levels up instruction in a way that is designed to bring ALL students to college and career readiness. We are used to accelerating instruction and infusing critical thinking for our top students. Now we need to do it for all students. Without equity and support, students who struggle could never engage in accelerated learning and critical thinking. At the same time, if all we provide is support and never accelerate learning, our ELLs, Standard English learners (SELs), and special education students are relegated to the back of the educational bus. They are stuck in low-track classes where they are

Figure 6.1 ACES Chart for Lesson Design

	Acceleration	Critical Thinking	Equity	Support
1	Instruction that identifies and builds on prior knowledge	Lesson Aim questions that require complex responses with no single correct answer	Rigorous curriculum designed to promote CCR[1] for all students	Structures in the classroom designed to meet the needs of struggling students, for example, Think-Pair-Share
2	Anticipation of learning errors (negative transfer)	Questions which check for understanding that are extended to prompt critical thinking	Activities that are student centered and require active processing by all	Integration of support techniques such as cue cards, WINK[2] sheets, scaffolded materials, and checkpoint deadlines
3	Inclusion of prior learning in practice activities to promote long-term retention	Lesson activities of increasing complexity	Jigsaw and other cooperative learning structures	Field notes taken and used to plan instruction
4	Compacting curriculum	Questions that require speculative responses	Instructional materials that are differentiated to engage all	Activities that include multiple modalities
5	Enrichment activities to deepen understanding	Questions or activities that require students to analyze	Assessment that is varied in form to highlight student strengths	Lessons that build the academic vocabulary of the curriculum
6	Assessment is used to inform instruction	Activities/projects that require judgment based on reason or evidence	Lessons/units that use different entry points, as identified by Howard Gardner	Support class lessons that are planned in collaboration with the general education teacher
7	Descriptions or exemplars of quality student work	Creative projects and assignments that require analysis and judgment	Choice in student assignments and activities	Lessons that include the active participation of the inclusion or other push-in teacher

1. College and career ready
2. What I Need to Know

drilled for whatever standardized test they are required to take. That is not what public schooling should be about.

This final chapter is designed to help the reader integrate the ACES into instruction and lesson design in a seamless way. The energy of the whole is greater than the parts. Some of what we have included in the preceding chapters are strategies that you, the reader, may already use. Other strategies may be new and challenge you to think differently about your practice. Our hope is that by organizing these strategies by ACES, you will think about them in an interconnected way as you design lessons that reflect the 2010 Common Core State Standards (CCSS) (National Governors Association, 2010) and Knowledge and Skills for University Success (KSUS) (Conley, 2003) standards.

We will present two lessons that take place over the course of several days and a one-day lesson that illustrates how the four ACES can be integrated. In order to make that integration clear to our readers, we have prepared a chart (Figure 6.1) that we will refer to as we describe each lesson by citing chart contents by letter and number, for example, A3. This will make the features of ACES that we are using transparent. Our chart is not meant to be an exhaustive list. It is a beginner's guide.

We invite our readers to make it their own and add to it as they practice ACES in lesson development. We also suggest that you use the chart to analyze your own lessons. Review your lessons to see which aspects of ACES they already contain. Groups of teachers working together on such an analysis would be a great staff development activity that would deepen understanding. We have included a protocol for staff development using ACES at the end of this chapter.

Model Lesson for High School Students:
Oral Literary Commentary

Present information, findings, and supporting evidence clearly, concisely, and logically such that listeners can follow the line of reasoning and the organization, development, substance, and style are appropriate to purpose, audience, and task.

National Governors Association, CCSS Curriculum: Speaking and Listening Standards, p. 50

(Continued)

(Continued)

Cite strong and thorough textual evidence to support analysis of what the text says explicitly as well as inferences drawn from the text.

National Governors Association, CCSS Curriculum: Reading Standards for Literature, p. 38

Are able to discuss with understanding the effects of an author's style and use of literary devices to influence the reader and evoke emotions. This includes devices such as imagery, characterization, choice of narrator, use of sound, formal and informal language, allusions, symbols, irony, voice, flashback, foreshadowing, time and sequence and mood.

Understanding University Success, pp. 22–23

Speaking in front of an audience is an emotionally trying experience. Nevertheless, being able to orally express your ideas and persuade others is one of the most important skills we can teach our students. Wisely, this skill was included in the Common Core State Standards (CCSS).

In order to give students the support that they need to be able to meet this standard, we suggest a series of lessons that integrate other CCSS and that culminate in an oral literary commentary. The oral presentation of the commentary can serve not only as a lesson, but as an authentic assessment of students' communicative skills and the mastery of related standards. It is this kind of assessment (not multiple-choice standardized tests) that should be used to measure college and career readiness.

A Literary Commentary

A literary commentary is an analysis of a passage. The analyzed work might come from a novel, a theatrical scene, a poem, or an essay. The commentary forces readers to do a close read of a text, to think about it deeply, and to create their own unique response to what they have read. Literary commentary is not an *I like this because* . . . as one might find in a book report. Instead, it draws upon the reader's know ledge of literature and literary devices and combines that with the reader's own unique encounter with the text. In an oral commentary, the student is asked to share his or her commentary with classmates so that a dialogue can begin and everyone's knowledge is deepened.

In many ways, an oral commentary is the culmination of what the CCSS and KSUS want students to be able to do—read closely, demonstrate understanding, develop a coherent argument, and use that argument to persuade others. The commentary goes up to the highest level of Bloom—students must create based on reason (C7) (Bloom, Ham, Melton, & O'Brient, 2001). This is indeed a "big elephant to eat" and therefore, students and teachers must begin by cutting it into little pieces. We will discuss those pieces before describing the lesson.

Close Reading and the Commentary

The need for students to do close reading is implicit in the CCSS (National Governors Association, 2010). If a student, for example, is able to "cite strong and thorough textual evidence to support analysis of what the text says explicitly as well as inferences drawn from the text" (p. 38), they demonstrate that they did a close reading of the text. When students do a close read of literature for commentary, they are reading with purpose—to notice features of the text such as structure, the use of literary elements, the development of theme or word choice, and so on.

Close reading is a skill that can be taught to any reader, even a reader who struggles. By manipulating the level of difficulty of the text (E4), students can engage in this higher level thinking skill of analysis (C5) without being thwarted by the materials.

According to Patricia Kain of the Harvard Writing Center (1998), students should begin a close reading with pen or pencil in hand. As they read, they annotate, by circling and underlining what strikes them as important or by making notes in margins. If the student is doing a close reading for commentary, she would underline words related to the idea or comments that she intends to develop. For example, if the student were doing a close reading to determine how an author uses religious symbols in a poem, the student would underline or circle what she believed were the religious symbols. On the side of the page, she might note the effect of their use on the reader.

(Continued)

(Continued)

In a close reading, students read (and think) like an investigator. Therefore, the second step is to look for patterns, contradictions, or surprises and to note them. Let's return to the example of close reading to identify the use of religious symbolism in a poem. The reader might identify whether all of the symbols are symbols associated with the same religion. She might look for secular symbols as well. The reader might ask why the author chose each symbol and what purpose it served. These observations then form the seeds of the commentary's argument.

Finally, students conclude the close reading (when its purpose is to develop a controlling idea) by asking questions based on their notes and the text. They choose one question on which to focus. For example, how does the author use religious symbolism to convey a message of social justice? The answer to that question would be the controlling idea on which each student builds her commentary.

With that background knowledge, let's jump into our ACES lesson.

Overarching Objective: The Creation of an Oral Commentary

The teacher realizes that teaching students to create and present an oral commentary will take time and require several developmental lessons. Her tenth-grade students have completed three literary works, *Lord of the Flies, Macbeth,* and *Frankenstein.* All three selections share common themes—the emergence of evil and the tension between good and evil impulses in humankind. She introduced the unit with the poem "After Experience Taught Me . . ." by W. D. Snodgrass (see the lesson in Chapter 4). For the commentary, the teacher would like her students to choose passages from one of the three studied works, do a close reading of a poem or passage with a related theme, and create the commentary with a controlling idea that is common to both. This will allow students to compare and contrast, a task that they are comfortable doing. It will also allow high achievers to take their commentary to a higher level if they choose—evaluate. The most skilled students will be able to argue which author more effectively responds to their controlling idea and why. The overarching objective that she creates is the following:

> *Students will create and present a commentary built upon a controlling idea that deepens understanding of two texts with related themes.*

This is certainly a tall order! Not only does it meet a CCSS, it is at the highest level of Bloom—create (Bloom et al., 2001). Our teacher now looks to the ACES chart, to see what aspects she is including in that objective. She quickly sees evidence of A1 and A5. She also sees that C1, C4, C5, C6, and C7, as well as E1, E2, E4, E5, and S4, are present.

She will now use the chart for its most helpful purpose. Those aspects not identified will help her design her lessons so that all students can be successful. The inclusion of as many aspects that are relevant and possible will guide her as she develops her lessons. That quick analysis shows her that she needs to integrate more activities from column *S* for support.

We will focus on the first lesson, how to create a controlling idea for a commentary, which we will describe in detail. As we describe each piece, we will make connections with Figure 6.1 in order to show how ACES is used in lesson design.

Objective: *Students will create a controlling idea for a commentary.*

Because her students were unfamiliar with the term *controlling idea* the teacher decided to accelerate their learning (A1) by building on a concept with which they were quite familiar—aim questions. She writes an aim question on the board every day. For this lesson, she posted the following Do Now activity on the board:

Open your notebook to your notes from February 3. How did you answer the following aim question for that day's lesson? Aim: What can we learn about the role of structure in the poem, "After Experience Taught Me . . ." by W. D. Snodgrass?

Because some students were absent the day the class read the poem or forgot to bring their notes to class, the teacher quickly paired unprepared students with prepared partners (S1). After a few moments, the teacher began a whole class share of their aim responses. The class concluded that although they read the same poem and answered the same question, their responses differed.

(Continued)

(Continued)

The teacher explained that having different answers that are all correct means that the aim question was a thought provoking question which required higher level thinking (C1). She then explained how a controlling idea for a commentary is just like an aim question for a lesson (A1). An aim gives a lesson focus and helps the learner understand what is to come. A controlling idea gives an essay focus and also explains what is to come in the essay. She described the purpose of a commentary, told the class that they would create a commentary, and gave her students a timeline for their work. The timeline explained the deliverables that were due along the way (S2). She lowered their concern by letting students know that support teachers will have all of the materials (S6), and she will work closely with them. She also told her students that much of the work will be done in class, that they will often work with partners (S1), and that she will differentiate materials so that everyone is challenged, but no one is overwhelmed (E4).

The students had practiced close readings, so they were familiar with the process (A1). For guided practice in creating a controlling idea for commentary, the teacher gave each student one of the following (E4):

The poem, "The Evil Seekers" by Anne Sexton (http://www.americanpoems.com/poets/annesexton/627)

or

The first paragraph of Chapter 10 of *The Strange Case of Dr. Jekyll and Mr. Hyde* by Robert Louis Stevenson (http://www.online-literature.com/stevenson/jekyllhyde/10/)

She gave *The Strange Case* to the class's most proficient readers because of its high level of difficulty (E4). Although she gave them the first paragraph, it was a full page in length and its vocabulary and sentence structure were very challenging. "The Evil Seekers" is rich in symbolism and meaning, but the vocabulary and structure are more approachable.

The teacher gave the students five minutes to silently read their assigned passages. The general education teacher and the inclusion teacher quietly gave support (S7) to readers who struggled with the text. They had prepared cue cards with Spanish translations of a few key words in the poem that the teachers thought the native Spanish speakers might not understand (S2). These were passed to students when needed.

When students were done reading, they did a quick Pair-Share with a partner who had the same assigned reading, and they responded to this question (S1): "What connection do you see between what you just read and one or more of the works that we studied in this unit?" Both teachers listened to student discussions and noted any misconceptions or misunderstandings that they heard (S3). They made note of any students who did not seem to understand their assigned reading so they could provide support during the next part of the lesson.

The students were now ready for their close reading. The teacher put the following terms on the board:

Language choice

Structure

Mood

Conflict

Tone

Theme

Students were told to think about their reading and choose one of the above (E7) as the lens for a close reading. As noted above, they had engaged in a close reading before. Students reread with pencil or pen in hand, noting examples of their chosen lens and commenting on its use. They were given ten minutes to complete the task (C5).

As the students worked, the teacher had a class roster with the choices listed. She noted the student choice of lens, and from that information, she created pairs.

After ten minutes, the teacher assigned partners based on common readings and lens choice (S1). She told the students that they and their assigned partners were to do the following:

Quickly compare notes.

Create a controlling idea based on their close reading.

She said, "You have just become an expert on your reading. If you were to teach others about it, what would be your aim question for that lesson?" She asked the students to write the question down. She then

(Continued)

(Continued)

asked the class to answer the question and write the answer down. She said, "The answer to the aim question is your controlling idea"(A1).

The teacher knew that she was asking students to make a leap, but she felt they were up for the challenge. She and the special education teacher had a model to share with any student pairs that were struggling (S2, S6). As they monitored pair progress, they observed that nearly all pairs were successful.

After five minutes, the teacher called the class together, reviewed several controlling ideas, and then assigned the homework. For homework, students were to list five pieces of evidence from the text to support their controlling idea.

Reflections on the Lesson and Next Steps

The teacher used about 50 percent of the ACES strategies in the lesson, which truly helped her level up the lesson with support. She will not abandon ACES in future lessons. Based on her and the coteacher's assessment of how students did in the Day 1 lesson (S3), as well as their knowledge of the students in the class, they will prepare packets for the commentary (E4). Some students will compare a passage from one of the three studied works with "After Experience Taught Me . . . ." That will be a good match for students who struggle with language and reading because they are quite familiar with the poem from the earlier analysis (A1, A3). Others will use "The **Evil Seekers**." This will be assigned to students who are ready to analyze a poem on their own, but cannot work with complex language. The most adept readers will work with the excerpt from *The Strange Case of Dr. Jekyll and Mr. Hyde*. This differentiation will bring variety to the presentations and, at the same time, allow students to get to the heart of the assignment, the oral commentary, without being frustrated by reading level (E1, E2, E4).

Although the teacher will let students choose the second work (E7) for the commentary—either *Lord of the Flies, Macbeth,* or *Frankenstein,* she will choose passages from each based on the lens they choose for their commentary and their second work. Although this is extra work for the teacher, it is time well spent (A4).

She has seen, time and again, how students can get so involved and frustrated by too much choice, they never get down to work. Second, she wants all of the focus to be on process for this first commentary so that they can truly engage in analysis and evaluation (A5). In Grades 11–12, students will become more independent in their selection (C3).

Finally, by limiting passages and lenses, students will be able to partner or work in small groups in their special education support classes, ELL classes, or English language arts (ELA) support classes (S6). All of the support teachers who are involved with the students can quickly come up to speed with the assignment and will have extra materials (as well as support materials) in their classes. She will tell the support teachers what student misunderstandings to look out for so those teachers can better support students as they work (A2).

When the teacher created the assignment, she also created the rubric for assessment (A6). During one lesson, the teacher shared recorded commentaries from the previous year that are exemplars (A7). The class discussed the rubric in detail. Half of the student's grade will be for process—diligence in class, in and out of class related assignments handed in on time, leadership and cooperation during group work, preparedness with notes and materials, and feedback from support teachers (E5). The teacher understands that by reinforcing the right behaviors, the final product will be better. The second half of the grade will be based on the commentary itself—how it is presented, its content, and the student's ability to respond to questions asked by classmates (S4, E5). Students used the rubric to discuss the sample commentaries and understand why they were highly rated by the teacher (A6).

A final consideration was given to students who were novices in English. The teacher understood how difficult oral presentations are for such students. With that in mind, she allowed the two ELL students who were beginners in their ability to speak English to do their presentation in the shelter of the ELL class (S6).

By the end of the unit, she used nearly all of the ACES strategies in Figure 6.1. Those that were not included were simply not needed for these lessons. There is no need to add a technique, just for the sake of including it. ACES is a toolbox and the tools must match the job at hand. The next lesson shows how ACES can be used in a very different lesson— a mathematics lesson for middle school students.

Model Lesson for Middle School Students: Using Ratio Reasoning and Proportionality to Solve Percent Problems

Understand ratio concepts and use ratio reasoning to solve problems.

National Governors Association,
CCSS for Mathematics, p. 42

Students extend their understanding of ratios and develop understanding of proportionality to solve single- and multi-step problems. Students use their understanding of ratios and proportionality to solve a wide variety of percent problems, including those involving discounts, interest, taxes, tips, and percent of increase or decrease. Students solve problems about scale drawings by relating corresponding lengths between the objects or by using the fact that relationships of lengths within an object are preserved in similar objects.

National Governors Association,
CCSS for Mathematics, p. 46

Understand the connections between proportional relationships, lines, and linear equations.

National Governors Association,
CCSS for Mathematics, p. 54

The CCSS above include standards from Grades 6–8 respectively. The concepts of ratio and proportion form the basis of a wide range of problem solving. These include measurement, percent, unit rate with ratios of fractions, unit pricing, and the slope of a graph. Each standard uses the word *understand* as the goal rather than *compute*, thus indicating the need for deep understanding. Too often teachers approach ratio and proportion as a mechanical computational skill, and they fail to take the time to develop the true power behind these concepts. Students must be given the opportunity to analyze the structure and meaning of a ratio and a proportion to fully appreciate and apply the concept to problems (C5). This lesson is designed to help students reach that deeper understanding on which to build their college and career ready skills (A5).

This Lesson Is for Grade 7

The teacher designed her lesson to achieve this objective in two class periods:

Students will use their understanding of ratios and proportionality to solve percent problems, including those involving taxes, tips, discounts, and percent of increase or decrease.

At first glance, this objective might seem too complex to tackle in that it includes four different types of problems. The traditional way to present this lesson is to develop it over the course of four days. Students would practice problems with taxes on Day 1, tips on Day 2, discounts on Day 3, and percent of increase and decrease on Day 4. In this ACES example, however, the teacher will compact the objective (A4) into two lessons by building on prior knowledge (A1) of percent, ratio, and proportion from sixth grade. She will also introduce a percent bar model that students can apply universally to any percent problem (S2, S4) instead of approaching each type of problem as unique and different (MathCamp, Inc., 2009).

To begin the lesson, the teacher wrote one word on the board for the Do Now activity:

PERCENT

She asked the students to write for three minutes to describe their understanding and experience with the word, *percent*. As the students wrote, the classroom teacher and the inclusion teacher (S7) monitored their writing. Students then traded papers with their partners (S1). The partner read the writing and underlined a sentence, phrase, or word that she found most interesting. The teacher selected ten students to read that phrase aloud, and she recorded their descriptive phrases on chart paper. The teacher clarified any misconceptions from the class and emphasized the consistent response that percent means *out of 100*. The teacher posed a simple problem with percent and asked the students to solve it using any strategy they choose (E7). Students were told to show their work, not just their answer.

In the school orchestra, 25% of the students play the violin. If there are 72 students in the orchestra, how many students play the violin?

(Continued)

(Continued)

As students worked independently, the classroom teacher and the inclusion teacher (S7) monitored the students. Students then shared their solution with their partners (S1). Solutions included dividing 72 by 4, multiplying .25 by 72, and setting up a proportion and solving. The teacher focused on the proportion. Most students knew that one ratio was 25/100 but the second ratio varied between x/72 and 72/x. Students commented that they weren't sure how to set up their *is over of* method.

At this teachable moment, the teacher introduced the percent bar as an alternative to the *is over of* method to eliminate the possibility of students relying on rote memorization without understanding (A2). She displayed the bars (see illustration below) and described each one.

The first bar was identified as 100 percent and labeled as the percent bar. The second bar of equal length was labeled *students*. Highlighting the fact that 100 percent is one whole, she asked students how many students were members of the **whole** orchestra. A student volunteered 72. The teacher asked the students where she should place the number 72 to be in sync with the percent bar. She gave students time to think about this. One student volunteered and placed 72 at the end of the student bar. The teacher reiterated that 100% and 72 both represented the whole. Students then considered where to place 25% on the percent bar, and one student drew a line approximately at the $\frac{1}{4}$ piece of the percent bar. The teacher asked, "As we lined up the 100% and 72, what number would correspond with the 25%. The students gave their answer of 18. The teacher asked, "Can we flip the numbers 18 and 72 placing the 72 at 25% and the 18 at 100%?" The students clearly saw the correct mathematical relationship (A2).

The teacher translated the two bars into two ratios, initially replacing 18 with x as that was the number that they were asked to find. She clarified the vocabulary words *ratio* and *proportion* by adding this to the model (S5). The mechanical calculations for solving for x were provided by the students starting with $100x = 25 \times 72$.

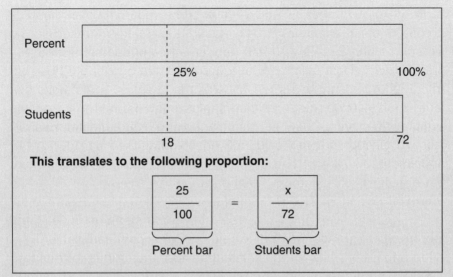

This translates to the following proportion:

$$\frac{25}{100} = \frac{x}{72}$$

Percent bar   Students bar

Students considered a second basic problem and were asked to use the percent bar to find the solution:

Maura has learned 21 of the 84 songs in her piano playbook. What percent of the total number of songs in the playbook has Maura learned?

The teacher and inclusion teacher (S7) offered assistance as needed. Students shared with their partners and one pair presented their solution to the class (A7). Again the teacher emphasized the placement of the 21 and 84.

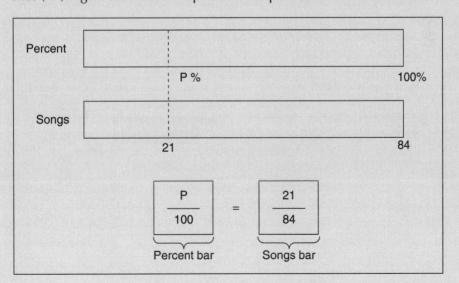

$$\frac{P}{100} = \frac{21}{84}$$

Percent bar   Songs bar

(Continued)

She then transferred the visual model to new applications (A1, C3). The teacher distributed two versions of problems differentiated by difficulty (E4). Each set included problems to address the objective of the lesson. The first set had the numbers included on the two bars for the initial two problems (S2), one on finding the tax and the second finding the tip. The students had to translate the bars to the ratios and solve. This set gradually built up to a higher level of difficulty (E1, C3). The second set included only more complex word problems and required the students to complete all steps without scaffolding (E4). This set also included problems that extended the learning to commission (A5, C2). An example of each type of problem is shown below. The students worked in homogeneous groups of four (E3). The teacher and the inclusion teacher assisted the groups as needed. Each group received a transparency of one of their problems to record the solution. These problems were common to each set of problems. Each group presented a problem to the class (E2).

Set 1 Problem

Trish and Juanita went out for dinner. They thought their food would cost $40 but needed to figure out the tax. If the tax rate is 8%, what is the tax on their food bill?

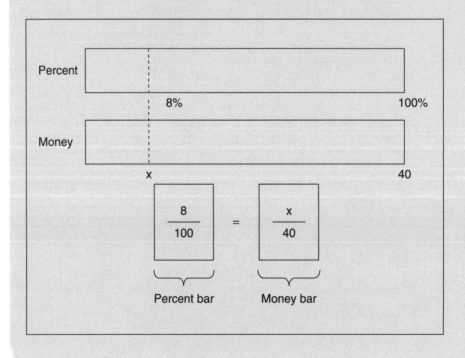

Set 2 Problem

Trish and Juanita were just finishing dinner at Dino's restaurant. The check arrived and when they went to pay, they were not sure if the tax was correct at $3.25. The check indicated $40 for their food. If the tax rate is 8.25% what is the tax on their food bill? Was the waiter correct in charging them $43.25 in total for dinner and tax?

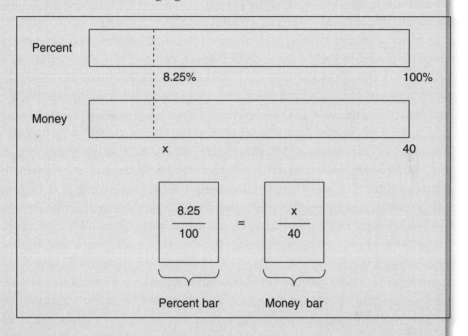

The homework assignment required the students to use the words: *percent, ratio,* and *proportion* in a paragraph of at least six sentences (S5). The ELL, SEL, and special education students were given an outline to use that included sentence starters (S2). For example, "Today I used a _____ bar to solve math problems."

Reflections on the Lesson and Next Steps

The teacher incorporated writing in the content area of mathematics in her Do Now activity (E6). Teachers of each content area, not just those teaching ELA, must include reading and writing strategies and activities in each unit of study to facilitate the learning of academic vocabulary in each subject area (Billmeyer & Barton, 1998). A directed free write provided a means of assessing each student's understanding of percent, the key vocabulary word (S5) for these lessons. This writing activity employed Gardner's 1993 research on multiple intelligences as it tapped linguistic intelligence (S4) and the foundational entry point (E6) by using written language and a key word to assess students' prior knowledge. When teachers of mathematics consistently use numerical or computational activities as a means to assess prior knowledge, they miss the opportunity to understand a student's conceptual understanding and may only see a lack of computational ability.

The teacher anticipated the common learning error from the *is over of* mechanical method and using the percent bar, she helped the students understand *why* this error is made (A2). The percent bar provided a schema, a mental and pictorial model for analyzing and solving percent problems. Students can link this model to their prior learning about percent and apply it going forward. Research by Jitendra et al., (2007) showed that students who learned word problem schemas in mathematics were more proficient in solving word problems than those who used keywords to solve a problem. They also concluded that students who learned a schema for solving math word problems retained the knowledge and transferred the knowledge to other situations.

The teacher was mindful of creating an equitable classroom. She addressed the range of math achievement in the classroom by effectively using the inclusion teacher (S7) and by differentiating the problem sets (E4). Although the difficulty and complexity of each set differed, each included examples to assess the lesson objective and ensure that each student met the CCSS (E1, C2). The homework assignment was open ended in that each student had to incorporate the academic vocabulary; however, some students used sentence starters to scaffold their thinking (E5). Sentence starters facilitate writing and understanding of academic vocabulary for students who struggle with language and literacy development (Calderon & Minaya-Rowe, 2011).

The lesson for the second day began with a small group share of the homework assignment. Each group was assigned one of the three vocabulary words—*percent, ratio,* or *proportion*—and had to select a sentence from the writings to share with the class (E3, A7). This is another effective sharing strategy for writing in content areas and building vocabulary within the regular classroom. In their book, *Teaching Reading in Mathematics,* Mary Lee Barton and Clare Heidema (2002) state that research studies have revealed that "a knowledge of mathematics vocabulary directly affects achievement in arithmetic, particularly in problem solving" (p. 21).

The teacher structured the second day's lesson with heterogeneous cooperative groups (E3). Problem sets included finding the discount, percent of decrease, and percent of increase at a Midnight Madness sale at a local appliance store. Each problem included the percent bar model, and some included a blank proportion to be completed. The problems with percent of decrease and percent of increase generated more than one way to use the percent bar (C5). Groups completed the first problem of finding discount and shared with the class:

PROBLEM 1

During the Midnight Madness sale, a large screen hi-def television that was originally priced at $1,260 was being reduced by 25%. If the television was discounted by 25%, how much was saved by making the purchase during the Midnight Madness sale?

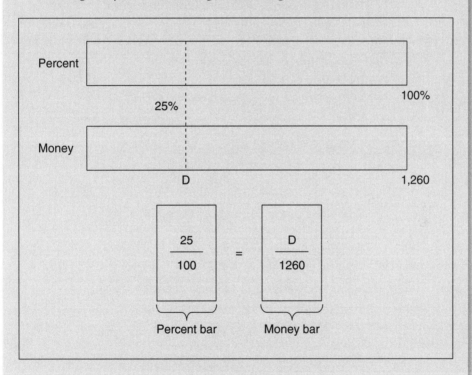

In the above problem and diagram, the teacher can extend the thinking by asking how much was paid for the television after receiving the discount (C2). The problem now uses 75% and moves the percent line to an approximate $\frac{3}{4}$ position on the percent and money bars. This lesson now moves on to problem 2.

(Continued)

(Continued)

PROBLEM 2

Last year there were 650 customers purchasing products during the Midnight Madness sale. This year there were 806 customers at the Midnight Madness sale. What is the percent of increase over last year's number of customers at the sale?

This problem could be solved using a variety of correct strategies, and therefore represents a wonderfully rich opportunity for students to share methods and to deepen each others' understanding of applying percents (A5).

The teacher structured the solution of the second problem relating to percent of increase by doing the following. First, groups set up their bars. Next, groups offered three different models and the rationale for the setup. Based on the bars, three different ratios were completed. Lastly, a group presented each solution to the class. One group found the percent of increase, *P*, (solution 2A) using $100 + P$ and 806 in the numerators of both terms of the proportion.

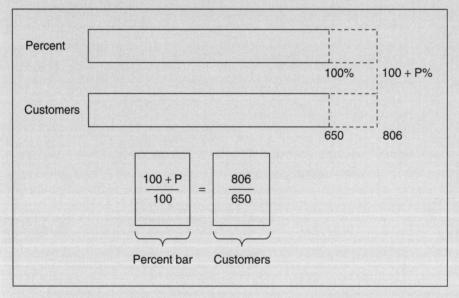

In solution 2B, some groups solved for *P* using only *P* and 806 in each numerator. This may appear initially as erroneous thinking as the result yields 124%. This became a wonderful opportunity for the class to explore this solution and deepen their understanding of exactly what *percent of increase* means (A5). Students recognized that they need to account for the amount greater than 100%, the percent of increase, to successfully answer the question.

Another group of students (Solution 2C) explored the problem by making a proportion based upon the numerators being the amounts of increase in each ratio: $806 - 650 = 156$ and $(100 + P) - 100 = P$.

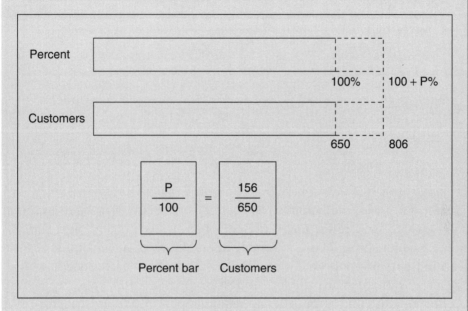

Groups completed two additional problems and shared their method and solution with the class. Homework was from the textbook and included five different percent word problems on finding the tax, tip, discount, percent of increase, and percent of decrease.

Application With Measurement

The CCSS for Mathematics states that students in Grade 6 must "Use ratio reasoning to convert measurement units" (National Governors Association (2010, p. 42). This concept is continued into Grade 7. The percent bar model can also be applied to measurement when students are converting measurements or using a scale drawing. The bars simply change to units of measure rather than percent; however, the structural thinking of using ratio reasoning and proportionality is the same as the percent model. Students find it helpful to write the units of measure in the first ratio as seen below C/M and then the correct units of measure line up for the solution. The same schema is applied (A1), thus linking new learning to prior knowledge (C1, C3):

The scale on a map of Tyrone's home state indicates that 1 centimeter is equivalent to 30 miles. On this map, the distance between Davenport and Vansburg is 12 centimeters. What is the actual distance between Davenport and Vansburg?

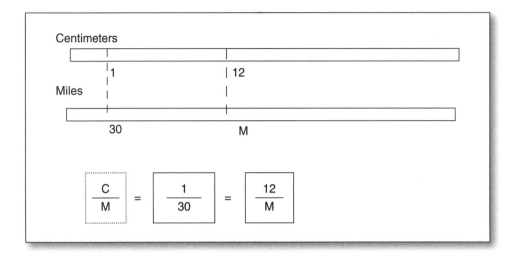

Middle school mathematics teachers devote many lessons to problem solving with unit rates, measurement units, ratio, percent, and proportional relationships. The bar model offers teachers a way to accelerate learning and promote retention. The method offers a consistent way to organize thinking with a deep understanding of ratio, ratio reasoning, proportionality, and proportional relationships. Students use the prior learning and apply the method to new situations.

Model Lesson Elementary: Informational Text in Grade 2

Ask and answer such questions as who, what, where, when, why, and how to demonstrate understanding of key details in a text.

Know and use various text features (e.g., captions, bold print, sub-headings, glossaries, indexes, electronic means, icons) to locate key facts or information in a text efficiently.

By the end of the year, read and comprehend informational texts, including history/social studies, science, and technical texts, in the grades 2-3 text complexity band proficiently, with scaffolding as needed at the high end of the range.

National Governors Association, CCSS Curriculum:
Reading Standards for Informational Text Grade 2, p. 13

> Write informative/explanatory texts in which they introduce a topic, use facts and definitions to develop points, and provide a concluding statement or section.
>
> National Governors Association, CCSS Curriculum:
> Writing Standards Grade 2, p. 19

Our final lesson is designed for students in the primary years. Second graders are fascinated with the world around them. They love to read books and listen to books about animals, sea creatures, insects, reptiles, unusual weather, and dinosaurs. When teaching science, teachers can use this high interest level to introduce students to reading informational texts and writing informative texts. Teachers must collect books on a specific topic with a range of reading levels and match books to the students' reading level (E4). Although students will read books of varying difficulty, all students will acquire the necessary knowledge about the topic, use nonfiction text features to locate facts, and compose a written informative piece (E1). Teachers typically share nonfiction books on a grade level, borrow from the library, and ask students to bring in books from their collections at home. The books should include text features as stated in the CCSS above, such as captions, bold print, subheadings, glossaries, and indexes, as well as table of contents, photographs, diagrams, and charts. Each text may not contain all of these features, but the format of the text must follow nonfiction structure.

If this is the students' first experience with an informational text, the teacher will model the use of the nonfiction text features prior to the first unit of study. Students should begin to develop an understanding of the genre and its purposes. A big book version of an appropriate text is ideal for this purpose. Each feature should be named and its purpose defined. Students are more familiar with fiction books and so a compare/contrast activity using a fiction and nonfiction text will help students better understand how to read a nonfiction text (A1, A3). In her book *A Curricular Plan for the Reading Workshop, Grade 2*, Lucy Calkins (2011) suggests comparing the reading routines for each genre. The goal for students is to read nonfiction with "fluency and intonation." She suggests teaching the students that "nonfiction readers read informational texts differently than we read stories, in part because the voice in our heads is different when we read nonfiction. Whereas stories have a story voice, nonfiction texts have the voice of a teacher or the narrator of a documentary" (p. 67).

(Continued)

(Continued)

As the teacher models reading a nonfiction text about toads, she can use a scaffolding web (Figure 6.2) to organize information from the text (S2). This will assist students in responding to the CCS standard to "answer such questions as who, what, where, when, why, and how to demonstrate understanding of key details in a text" (p. 13). As the teacher completes the web with the students, she highlights how the use of text features helps them find the details about the topic. For example, to answer the web section, *when* do they eat, the teacher uses the index, finds the word *food* with the page number, and demonstrates how to find the information. Students name other facts about the topic that are written at the bottom of the web.

Figure 6.2 Scaffolding Web

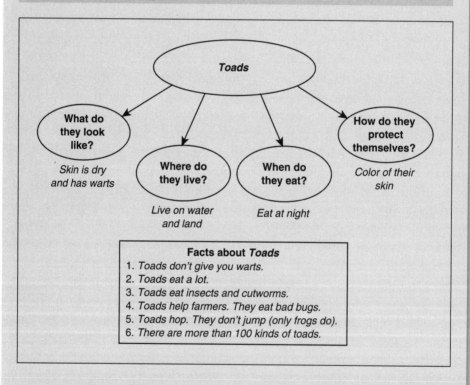

This model is then applied to the second-grade science unit on ladybugs. The teacher, using input from the special education and ELL teachers (S7), matches each student with a book on ladybugs. Each student reads the book independently or with a partner and assistant and then completes the graphic organizer following the teacher model. The teacher(s) and support assistant(s) offer help as needed. Students now share facts and insights about the topic thus enlarging the overall knowledge base of the class (S4).

The teacher can offer a variety of writing formats for students to demonstrate their understanding of the topic (E5). Students choose a writing task (E7) and must include at least four facts about ladybugs (C6). Students can write a first person poem, taking on the persona of a ladybug, "I Am a Ladybug" or write a short book, *Ladybugs Are Lovely* or *I Wish I Were a Ladybug*, for example. They might choose to create a similar picture book, having more pictures and less text. They could create a hanger mobile showing different facts about ladybugs, create a board game with pictures and facts, or write a letter to larvae describing the next phase of life. The possibilities are only limited by the teacher's and children's imagination (C3, S2, S4).

Students share their writing with the class (A7). Using the plethora of information about ladybugs, the teacher introduces the structure of an informative paragraph based on the CCSS. The teacher "shares the pen" with her students and together they create an introductory sentence. For example, *Ladybugs are colorful beetles with BIG appetites.* Each student, with a partner, copies the introductory sentence onto lined paper. Students then work with partners to write three facts for the paragraph. The teacher and support staff pair struggling students with more-able students (S1). The teachers circulate to work with each pair. The teacher again shares the pen as the class creates a concluding statement. For example, *Ladybug, ladybug, keep saving our plants.* If feasible, the teacher can purchase ladybug larvae for the classroom for students to experience firsthand the life cycle of the ladybug (E6). This will generate many questions and speculative comments that will be answered as students glean facts from their books. Interested students can further explore information about ladybugs—for example, how farmers named this beetle a *ladybug* after the biblical Mary, whom they called Our Lady. They prayed to her, and their crops were saved from insects. Or students might want to research the history behind the rhyme "Ladybug, Ladybug fly away home"(C7).

For future science or social studies units, the teacher can follow a similar format but gradually move students to independence when they write their own informative paragraph.

After prior lessons, there was a reflection. This time, we invite our readers to follow the process that we have used.

- Explain how each aspect of ACES was used in the lesson.
- What other aspects of ACES could be incorporated to even further improve the lesson by accelerating learning, embedding critical thinking, using equitable practices, and providing support?

USING ACES TO BUILD YOUR OWN LESSONS

Creating lessons that effectively use ACES will take time. We suggest that teachers begin by developing a deep understanding of the model with others, gradually moving to their own independent practice. School leaders should be part of the process as well so that both teachers and those who supervise instruction work together for the benefit of students. Below is a simple professional development protocol that we suggest. Please note, what we outline below should take place over the course of months. As simple as it is, it is not intended to be a single day's professional development activity.

Protocol for Professional Development Using ACES

Step 1: Using the chart in Figure 6.1, analyze the lessons in Chapters 2–5. Identify where and how ACES were used in the lesson. What revisions could be incorporated to incorporate ACES even further?

Step 2: Each member of the study group should bring two of their own lessons to serve as sample lessons. Now use the chart to analyze those lessons.

Are all four principles (*A, C, E,* and *S*) present in the lesson?

Is there balance among the four?

How could we change the lesson to better incorporate ACES?

The group revises the lesson.

Step 3: Have one member of the group teach the revised lesson while the others observe the learners in the class. The observers take field notes based on a group-developed protocol.

Step 4: Evaluate the effectiveness of the lesson on the group-created criteria, such as quality of student work and the active engagement of students. Discuss how the incorporation of ACES affected what you observed. What might you change in the lesson?

Step 5: Reteach, observe, discuss.

USING ACES TO DEVELOP CURRICULUM

The curriculum for any subject should be a dynamic document designed by teachers in conjunction with administrators. This document becomes the essential tool in designing lessons. As one of our teachers mentioned when referring to her curriculum, "This is my bible." Teachers will believe this statement if the curriculum reflects the collective wisdom of a department or grade level as well as a synthesis of best practices and instructional beliefs (Burris & Garrity, 2008).

We have included a curriculum template in Resource A. A suggested timeframe is essential for each unit of study to ensure that instructional time is not wasted on repetitive lessons from previously taught objectives. Instead, new learning builds on prior learning. The template fleshes out each unit of study and includes the following elements:

- Learning objectives
- CCS and KSUS standards (A)
- Levels of Bloom's Taxonomy based on the learning objective (C)
- Differentiated teaching resources (E)
- Content area reading and writing activities (S)

Figure 3.6 will be useful for teachers to identify the level of Bloom's Taxonomy.

CLOSING THOUGHTS

The question of readiness, which we grapple with today, is not a new one. In the conclusion to our previous book, we told the story of the Committee of Ten (Burris & Garrity, 2008). It is a story worth telling again. In 1892, the National Education Association's Committee of Ten was given the mission of creating criteria for college acceptance. They were also charged with determining how the public schools of the time should best prepare students for a college education. More students than ever before had access to high school. According to educational historian Herbert Kliebard (1995), the committee was steadfast in its belief that all students "were entitled to the best ways of teaching the various subjects" and that "education for life" is "education for college" (p. 11).

Over a century ago, the Committee of Ten knew that college and career readiness were one and the same. As they held firm in their belief, they were criticized by those who believed that our immigrants and working poor were a "great army of incapables", and that college readiness should be designed for the few not the many.

The chairman of the committee was the president of Harvard University, Charles W. Eliot. He did not believe that it was the mission of public schools to sort and select students into different curricula based on student background or a schoolmaster's perception of what path students should take in life. Eliot (1905) asked the key rhetorical question, "Who are we to make these prophecies?" (as cited in Kliebard, p. 331).

He was, of course, right. It is not ours to decide who goes to college and who does not. It is our responsibility, instead, to prepare all of the students with whom we are entrusted to freely make choices. They can have that freedom if, and only if, we give them the skills and the knowledge that enables them to choose. If the Common Core State Standards stay true to this guiding principle and not become ensnared in testing, then it will stay true to the principles of the Committee of Ten and their democratic ideals.

It is in that spirit that we wrote this book. We hope you find it helpful on your journey to open the Common Core to all and ensure equitable excellence in your classrooms.

Resource: Curriculum Template

Unit of study: _____ Time allotted: _____

Learning Objective	CCS Standard	Level of Bloom's Taxonomy	Differentiated Teaching Resources	Reading/Writing Strategies

References

Achieve and the Education Trust. (2008). *Making college and career readiness the mission for high schools: A guide for state policymakers.* Retrieved from http://www.txccrs.org/downloads/Achieve_MakingCCRtheMission.pdf

Adelman, C. (1999). *Answers in the tool box: Academic intensity, attendance patterns, and bachelor's degree attainment.* Washington, DC: U.S. Department of Education, Office of Educational Research. Retrieved from http://www2.ed.gov/pubs/Toolbox/index.html

Alliance for Excellent Education. (2005). *Six key strategies for teachers of English language learners.* Retrieved from http://www.all4ed.org/files/archive/publications/SixKeyStrategies.pdf

Ames, M. (2010). What happens to students once they're in college. *Newsleader, 57*(5), 6.

Anderson, L. W., & Krathwohl, D. R. (Eds.). (2001). *A taxonomy for learning, teaching and assessing: A revision of Bloom's Taxonomy of educational objectives: Complete edition.* New York: Longman.

Barton, M. L., & Heidema, C. (2002). *Teaching reading in mathematics* (2nd ed.). Aurora, CO: McREL.

Billmeyer, R., & Barton, M. L. (1998). *Teaching reading in the content areas: If not me, then who?* (2nd ed.) Aurora, CO: McREL.

Bloom, B. S. (1968). Learning for mastery. *Evaluation comment 1*(2). The Center for the Study of Evaluation of Instructional Programs: The University of California at Los Angeles.

Bloom, B. S. (Ed.), Engelhart, M. D., Furst, E. J., Hill, W. H., & Krathwohl, D. R. (1956). *Taxonomy of educational objectives: The classification of educational goals. Handbook 1: Cognitive domain.* White Plains, NY: Longman.

Bloom, H. S., Ham, S., Melton, L., & O'Brient, J. (2001). *Evaluating the accelerated schools approach: A look at early implementation and impacts on student achievement in eight elementary schools.* New York, NY: Manpower Demonstration Research Corporation.

Boulware-Gooden, R., Carreker, S., Thornhill, A., & Joshi, R. M. (2007). Instruction of metacognitive strategies enhances reading comprehension and vocabulary achievement of third-grade students. *The Reading Teacher, 61*(1), 70–77.

Braddock, J. H., II, & Dawkins, M. P. (1993). Ability grouping, aspirations, and attainment: Evidence from the National Educational Longitudinal Study of 1988. *Journal of Negro Education, 62*, 324–336.

Bransford, J., Brown, A., & Cocking, R. (1999). *How people learn: Brain, mind, experience, and school.* Washington, DC: National Academy Press.

Brown, J. E., & Doolittle, J. (2008). *A cultural, linguistic, and ecological framework for response to intervention with English language learners.* Retrieved from http://www.niusileadscape.org/docs/FINAL_PRODUCTS/LearningCarousel/Framework_for_RTI_with_ELLs.pdf

Burstein, L. (1993). Studying learning, growth and instruction cross nationally: Lessons learned in why and why not engage in cross-national studies. *The IEA study of mathematics III: Student growth and classroom processes.* Oxford, UK: Pergamon.

Burris, C. C., & Garrity, D. T. (2009). Equity and excellence. *The American School Board Journal, 196*(1), 29–31.

Burris, C. C., & Garrity, D. T. (2008). *Detracking for excellence and equity.* Alexandria, VA: ASCD.

Burris, C. C., Heubert, J., & Levin, H. (2006). Accelerating mathematics achievement using heterogeneous grouping. *American Educational Research Journal, 43*(1), 103–134.

Burris, C. C., Heubert, J., & Levin, H. (2004). Math acceleration for all. *Educational Leadership, 66*(5), 68–71.

Burris, C. C., & Welner, K. G. (2005). Closing the achievement gap by detracking. *Phi Delta Kappan, 86*(8), 594–598.

Burris, C. C., Welner, K., Wiley, E., & Murphy, J. (2008). Accountability, rigor, and detracking: Achievement effects of embracing a challenging curriculum as a universal good for all students. *Teachers College Record, 110*(3), 571–607.

Calderon, M., & Minaya-Rowe, L. (2011). *Preventing long-term ELs: Transforming schools to meet core standards.* Thousand Oaks, CA: Corwin.

Calkins, L. (2011). *A curricular plan for the reading workshop, grade 2.* Portsmouth, NH: Heinemann.

Carnegie Forum on Education and the Economy. (1986). *A nation prepared: Teachers for the 21st century.* Washington, DC: Carnegie Forum on Education and the Economy.

Chokshi, S., & Fernandez, C. (2005). Reaping the systemic benefits of lesson study: Insights for the U.S. *Phi Delta Kappan, 86*(5), 674–680.

Clark, C., & Fifer, N. (1999). *Poetry in six dimensions: 20th century voices.* Cambridge, MA: Educators Publishing Service.

Clark, K. F., & Graves, M. F. (2005). Scaffolding students' comprehension of text. *The Reading Teacher, 58*(11), 570–580.

College Board. (2009). *Facts for education advocates: International comparisons.* Retrieved from http://connection-collegeboard.com/09jan/advocacy_facts.html

Conley, D. T. (2003). *Understanding university success: A report from standards for success.* Eugene, OR: Center for Educational Policy Research.

Darling-Hammond, L. (2010). The flat world and education: How American's commitment to equity will determine our future. New York, NY: Teachers College Press.

Darling-Hammond, L., & Wise, A. E. (1992). Teacher professionalism. In M. Alkin (Ed.), *Encyclopedia of educational research* (6th ed.), (Vol. 1), (pp. 1359–1366). New York, NY: Macmillan.

Dewey, J. (1879). My pedagogic creed. *The School Journal, 54,* 77–80.

Diaz-Rico, L. T., & Weed, K. Z. (2002). *The crosscultural language and academic development handbook* (2nd ed.). Boston, MA: Allyn and Bacon.

Dillon, S. (2009, October, 8). Study finds a high rate of imprisonment among dropouts. *The New York Times.* Retrieved from http://www.nytimes.com/2009/10/09/education/09dropout.html

Echevarria, J., & Hasbrouck, J. (2009). *Response to intervention and English learners.* Retrieved from http://www.cal.org/create/resources/pubs/CREATEBrief_ResponsetoIntervention.pdf

Fernandez, C. (2002). Learning from Japanese approaches to professional development: The case of lesson study. *Journal of Teacher Education, 53*(5), 393–405.

Finnan, C., & Swanson, J. D. (2000). *Accelerating the learning of all students.* Boulder, CO: Westview Press.

Finnan C., St. John, E. P., McCarthy, J., & Slovacek, S. P. (1996). *Accelerated schools in action: Lessons from the field.* Thousand Oaks, CA: Corwin.

Finnish National Board of Education. (2004). *Background for Finnish PISA success.* Retrieved from http://www.edu.fi/english/page.asp?path=500,571,36263

Freeman, Y. S., & Freeman, D. E. (2009). *Academic language for English language learners and struggling readers.* Portsmouth, NH: Heinemann.

Gardner, H. (1993). *Multiple intelligences: The theory in practice.* New York, NY: Basic Books.

Garrity, D. (2004). Detracking with vigilance. *School Administrator, 61*(7), 24–27.

Garrity, D. T., & Burris, C. C. (2007). Personalized learning in detracked classrooms. *School Administrator, 64*(8), 10–16.

George, P. (1992). *How to untrack your school.* Alexandria, VA: Association for Supervision and Curriculum Development.

Handerwork, P., Tognatta, N., Coley, R., & Gittomer, D. (2008). *Access to success: Patterns of advanced placement participation in US high schools.* Educational Testing Service. Retrieved from http://www.ets.org/Media/Research/pdf/PIC-ACCESS.pdf

Harvey, S., & Goudvis, A. (2000). *Strategies that work.* Portland, ME: Stenhouse.

Haynes, J., & Zacarian, D. (2010). *Teaching English language learners across the content areas.* Alexandria, VA: ASCD.

Heubert, J. P. (2002). First do no harm: How the misuse of promotion and graduation tests hurts our neediest students. *Educational Leadership, 60*(4), 26–31.

Holmes Group. (1986). *Tomorrow's teachers.* East Lansing: Michigan State University.

Hunter, M. (1982). *Mastery teaching.* Thousand Oaks, CA: Corwin.

Hurwitz, J. (1987). *Class clown.* New York, NY: Scholastic.

Individuals with Disabilities Education Act of 2004 (IDEA). (2004). Public Law 108–446.

Jitendra, A. K., Griffin, C. C., Haria, P., Leh, J., Adams, A., & Kaduvettoor, A. (2007). A comparison of single and multiple strategy instruction on third-grade students' mathematical problem solving. *Journal of Educational Psychology, 99*(1), 115–127.

Joosse, B. (1991). *Mama, do you love me?* San Francisco, CA: Chronicle.

Kain, P. (1998). *How to do a close reading.* Retrieved from http://www.fas.harvard.edu/~wricntr/documents/CloseReading.html

Khadaroo, S. T. (2011). *Civil rights survey: 3,000 US high schools don't have math beyond Algebra 1.* Retrieved from http://www.csmonitor.com/USA/Education/2011/0630/Civil-rights-survey-3-000-US-high-schools-don-t-have-math-beyond-Algebra-I

Kifer, E., Wolfe, R. G., & Schmidt, W. H. (1993). Understanding patterns of student growth. In L. Burstein (Ed.), *The IEA study of mathematics III: Student growth and classroom processes* (pp. 101–127). Oxford, UK: Pergamon.

Kliebard, H. M. (1995). *The struggle for the American curriculum: 1893–1958* (2nd ed.). New York, NY: Routledge.

Krathwohl, D. R. (2002). A revision of Bloom's Taxonomy: An overview. *Theory into Practice 41*(4), 212–218.

Levin, H. M. (1988). *Accelerated schools for at-risk students* (Report No. 142). New Brunswick, NJ: Rutgers University.

Levin, Henry M. (1987). *New schools for the disadvantaged.* Aurora, CO: Mid-continent Regional Educational Lab. Retrieved from http://www.eric.ed.gov/PDFS/ED310176.pdf

Lucas, S. R. (1999). *Tracking inequality: Stratification and mobility in American high schools.* New York, NY: Teachers College Press.

MathCamp, Inc. (2009). *Of taxes and tips -Bar model.* Retrieved from http://math-camp.com/display.php?Page=1

MathCamp, Inc. (2006). *WINK sheet shell.* Retrieved from http://mathcamp.com/display.php?Page=16

MathCamp, Inc. (2005). *The box method of multiplying binomials.* Retrieved from http://mathcamp.com/display.php?Page=13

Mayer, R. E. (2002). *Teaching for meaningful learning.* Upper Saddle River, NJ: Prentice Hall.

Mayer, R. E. (1992). *Thinking, problem solving, cognition* (2nd ed.). New York, NY: Freeman.

Mellard, D. F., & Johnson, E. (2008). *RTI: A practitioner's guide to implementing response to intervention.* Thousand Oaks, CA: Corwin.

Mickelson, R. (2001). Subverting Swann: First- and second-generation segregation in Charlotte-Mecklenburg schools. *American Educational Research Journal, 38,* 215–252.

National Governors Association Center for Best Practices and Council of Chief State School Officers. (2010). *Common core state standards initiatives: Preparing America's students for college and career.* Retrieved from http://www.corestand-ards.org/

National Research Council. (1991). *In the mind's eye: Enhancing human performance.* Daniel Druckman and Robert A. Bjork (Eds.). Washington, DC: National Academy Press.

National Research Council and the Institute of Medicine. (2004). *Engaging schools: Fostering high school students' motivation to learn.* Washington, DC: National Academy Press.

Oakes, J. (2005). *Keeping track: How schools structure inequality* (2nd ed.). New Haven, CT: Yale University.

Obama, B. (2011, January 25). *The state of the union address.* Retrieved from http://abcnews.go.com/Politics/State_of_the_Union/state-of-the-union-2011-full-transcript/story?id=12759395

OECD. (2009). *Trends in tertiary graduation and entry rates.* Paris, France: OECD. Retrieved from http://titania.sourceoecd.org/vl=1710423/cl=20/nw=1/rpsv/factbook2009/09/01/02/index.htm

Orfield, G., & Lee, C. (2006). *Racial transformation and the changing nature of segregation.* Cambridge, MA: The Civil Rights Project at Harvard University. Retrieved from http://www.civilrightsproject.ucla.edu/research/deseg/deseg06.php

Ovando, C., Collier, V., & Combs, M. (2003). *Bilingual and ESL classrooms: Teaching multicultural contexts* (3rd ed.). Boston, MA: McGraw-Hill.

Peterson, J. M. (1989). Remediation is no remedy. *Educational Leadership, 46*(6), 24–25.

Pintrich, P. R. (2002). The role of metacognitive knowledge in learning, teaching, and assessing. *Theory into Practice 41*(4), 219–225.

Polacco, P. (2001). *The keeping quilt.* St. Louis, MO: Turtleback Books.

Porter, A., McMaken, J., Hwang, J., & Yang, R. Common core standards: The new U.S. intended curriculum. *Educational Researcher 40*(3), 103–116.

Pugalee, D. K. (2001). Writing, mathematics, and metacognition: Looking for the connections through students' work in mathematical problem solving. *School Science and Mathematics, 101*(5), 236–245.

Raths, J. (2002). Improving instruction. *Theory into Practice 41*(4), 233–237.

Rea, D. M., & Mercuri, S. P. (2006). *Research-based strategies for English language learners: How to reach goals and meet standards, K-8.* Portsmouth, NH: Heinemann.

Reis, S. M. (n.d.). *Research that supports using the schoolwide enrichment model and extensions of gifted education pedagogy to meet the needs of all students.* Retrieved from http://www.gifted.uconn.edu/sem/semresearch.html

Reis, S. M., Gentry, M., & Maxfield, L. R. (1998). The application of enrichment clusters to teachers' classroom practices. *Journal for Education of the Gifted, 21,* 310–324.

Robb, L. (2006). *Teaching reading.* New York, NY: Scholastic.

Robb, L. (2003). *Teaching reading in social studies, science, and math.* New York, NY: Scholastic.

Robb, L. (2000). *Teaching reading in the middle school.* New York, NY: Scholastic.

Rohrer, D., & Pashler, H. (2010). Recent research on human learning challenges conventional instructional strategies. *Educational Researcher, 39*(5), 406–412.

Slavin, R. E. (1991). Synthesis of research of cooperative learning. *Educational Leadership, 48*(5), 71–82.

Slavin, R., & Braddock, J., III. (1993). Ability grouping: On the wrong track. *College Board Review, 168,* 11–17.

Snodgrass, W. D. (1987). After Experience taught me . . . . *Selected poems 1957–1987.* New York, NY: Soho.

Stigler, J., & Hiebert, J. (1999). *The teaching gap—Best ideas from the world's teachers for improving education in the classroom.* New York, NY: The Free Press.

Sullivan, D., & O'Neil, M. A. (1980). This is us! Great graphs for kids. *Arithmetic Teacher, 28*(1), 14–18.

Thompson, C. J. (2009) Preparation, practice and performance: An empirical examination of the impact of standards based instruction on secondary students' math and science achievement. *Research in Education, 81,* 53–62.

Useem, E. L. (1992). Middle schools and math groups: Parents' involvement in children's placement. *Sociology of Education, 65,* 263–279.

Vaughn, S. (2011). *Response to intervention and English learners.* Retrieved from http://www.rtinetwork.org/learn/diversity/englishlanguagelearners

Weinstein, C. E., & Mayer, R. (1986). The teaching of learning strategies. In M. C. Wittrock (Ed.), *Handbook of research on teaching* (pp. 315–327). New York, NY: Macmillan.

Welner, K. G. (2001). *Legal rights, local wrongs: When community control collides with educational equity.* Albany, NY: SUNY Press.

White, P., Gamoran, A., Porter, A. C., & Smithson, J. (1996). Upgrading the high school math curriculum: Math course-taking patterns in seven high schools in California and New York. *Educational Evaluation and Policy Analysis, 18,* 285–307.

Zweirs, J. (2008). *Building academic language: Essential practices for content classrooms.* San Francisco, CA: Jossey-Bass.

Index

CORWIN

A SAGE Company

The Corwin logo—a raven striding across an open book—represents the union of courage and learning. Corwin is committed to improving education for all learners by publishing books and other professional development resources for those serving the field of PreK–12 education. By providing practical, hands-on materials, Corwin continues to carry out the promise of its motto: **"Helping Educators Do Their Work Better."**